with

Windows XP

Getting Started

Shelley Gaskin, Robert L. Ferrett,

John Preston, and Sally Preston

Upper Saddle River, New Jersey

This book is dedicated to my students, who inspire me every day, and to my husband, Fred Gaskin.
—Shelley Gaskin

We dedicate this book to our granddaughters, who bring us great joy and happiness: Clara and Siena & Alexis and Grace.
—John Preston, Sally Preston, and Robert L. Ferrett

Library of Congress Cataloging-in-Publication Data

Go! Getting started with Windows XP / Shelley Gaskin . . . [et al.].
p. cm.
Includes index.
ISBN 0-13-231839-3
1. Microsoft Windows (Computer file) 2. Operating systems (Computers) I. Gaskin, Shelley.
QA76.76.O63G6 2007
005.4'46--dc22
2007009635

Vice President and Publisher: Natalie E. Anderson
Associate VP/Executive Acquisitions Editor, Print: Stephanie Wall
Executive Acquisitions Editor, Media: Richard Keaveny
Product Development Manager: Eileen Bien Calabro Sr.
Editorial Project Manager: Laura Burgess
Development Editor: Ginny Munroe
Editorial Assistants: Becky Knauer, Lora Cimiluca
Content Development Manager: Cathi Profitko
Production Media Project Manager: Lorena Cerisano
Senior Media Project Manager: Steve Gagliostro
Director of Marketing: Margaret Waples
Senior Marketing Manager: Jason Sakos
Sales Associate: Rebecca Scott
Managing Editor: Lynda J. Castillo
Production Project Manager/Buyer: Wanda Rockwell
Production Editor: GGS Book Services
Photo Researcher: GGS Book Services
Manufacturing Buyer: Natacha Moore
Production/Editorial Assistant: Sandra K. Bernales
Design Director: Maria Lange
Art Director/Interior Design: Blair Brown
Cover Photo: Courtesy of Getty Images, Inc./Marvin Mattelson
Composition: GGS Book Services
Project Management: GGS Book Services
Cover Printer: Phoenix Color
Printer/Binder: Courier Kendallville

10
ISBN-10: 0-13-231839-3
ISBN-13: 978-0-13-231839-6

Table of Contents

Letter from the Editor

Dear Instructors and Students,

The primary goal of the *GO!* Series is two-fold. The first goal is to help instructors teach the course they want in less time. The second goal is to provide students with the skills to solve business problems using the computer as a tool, for both themselves and the organization for which they might be employed.

The *GO!* Series was originally created by Series Editor Shelley Gaskin and published with the release of Microsoft Office 2003. Her ideas came from years of using textbooks that didn't meet all the needs of today's diverse classroom and that were too confusing for students. Shelley continues to enhance the series by ensuring we stay true to our vision of developing quality instruction and useful classroom tools.

But we also need your input and ideas.

Over time, the *GO!* Series has evolved based on direct feedback from instructors and students using the series. *We are the publisher that listens.* To publish a textbook that works for you, it's critical that we continue to listen to this feedback. It's important to me to talk with you and hear your stories about using *GO!* Your voice can make a difference.

My hope is that this letter will inspire you to write me an e-mail and share your thoughts on using the *GO!* Series.

Stephanie Wall
Executive Editor, *GO!* Series
stephanie_wall@prenhall.com

GO! System Contributors

We thank the following people for their hard work and support in making the *GO!* System all that it is!

Additional Author Support

Coyle, Diane	Montgomery County Community College
Fry, Susan	Boise State
Townsend, Kris	Spokane Falls Community College
Stroup, Tracey	Amgen Corporation

Instructor Resource Authors

Amer, Beverly	Northern Arizona University
Boito, Nancy	Harrisburg Area Community College
Coyle, Diane	Montgomery County Community College
Dawson, Tamara	Southern Nazarene University
Driskel, Loretta	Niagara County Community College
Elliott, Melissa	Odessa College
Fry, Susan	Boise State
Geoghan, Debra	Bucks County Community College
Hearn, Barbara	Community College of Philadelphia
Jones, Stephanie	South Plains College
Madsen, Donna	Kirkwood Community College
Meck, Kari	Harrisburg Area Community College
Miller, Cindy	Ivy Tech
Nowakowski, Tony	Buffalo State
Pace, Phyllis	Queensborough Community College
Paterson, Jim	Paradise Valley Community College
Prince, Lisa	Missouri State
Rodgers, Gwen	Southern Nazarene University
Ruymann, Amy	Burlington Community College
Ryan, Bob	Montgomery County Community College
Smith, Diane	Henry Ford College
Spangler, Candice	Columbus State Community College
Thompson, Joyce	Lehigh Carbon Community College
Tiffany, Janine	Reading Area Community College
Watt, Adrienne	Douglas College
Weaver, Paul	Bossier Parish Community College
Weber, Sandy	Gateway Technical College
Wood, Dawn	
Weissman, Jonathan	Finger Lakes Community College

Super Reviewers

Brotherton, Cathy	Riverside Community College
Cates, Wally	Central New Mexico Community College
Cone, Bill	Northern Arizona University
Coverdale, John	Riverside Community College
Foster, Nancy	Baker College
Helfand, Terri	Chaffey College
Hibbert, Marilyn	Salt Lake Community College
Holliday, Mardi	Community College of Philadelphia
Jerry, Gina	Santa Monica College
Martin, Carol	Harrisburg Area Community College
Maurer, Trina	Odessa College
Meck, Kari	Harrisburg Area Community College
Miller, Cindy	Ivy Tech Community College
Nielson, Phil	Salt Lake Community College
Rodgers, Gwen	Southern Nazarene University
Smolenski, Robert	Delaware Community College
Spangler, Candice	Columbus State Community College
Thompson, Joyce	Lehigh Carbon Community College
Weber, Sandy	Gateway Technical College
Wells, Lorna	Salt Lake Community College
Zaboski, Maureen	University of Scranton

Technical Editors

Janice Snyder
Joyce Nielsen
Colette Eisele
Janet Pickard
Mara Zebest
Lindsey Allen
William Daley

Student Reviewers

Allen, John	Asheville-Buncombe Tech Community College
Alexander, Steven	St. Johns River Community College
Alexander, Melissa	Tulsa Community College
Bolz, Stephanie	Northern Michigan University
Berner, Ashley	Central Washington University
Boomer, Michelle	Northern Michigan University
Busse, Brennan	Northern Michigan University
Butkey, Maura	Central Washington University
Christensen, Kaylie	Northern Michigan University
Connally, Brianna	Central Washington University
Davis, Brandon	Northern Michigan University
Davis, Christen	Central Washington University
Den Boer, Lance	Central Washington University
Dix, Jessica	Central Washington University
Moeller, Jeffrey	Northern Michigan University
Downs, Elizabeth	Central Washington University
Erickson, Mike	Ball State University
Gadomski, Amanda	Northern Michigan University
Gyselinck, Craig	Central Washington University
Harrison, Margo	Central Washington University
Heacox, Kate	Central Washington University
Hill, Cheretta	Northwestern State University
Innis, Tim	Tulsa Community College
Jarboe, Aaron	Central Washington University
Klein, Colleen	Northern Michigan University
Moeller, Jeffrey	Northern Michigan University
Nicholson, Regina	Athens Tech College
Niehaus, Kristina	Northern Michigan University
Nisa, Zaibun	Santa Rosa Community College
Nunez, Nohelia	Santa Rosa Community College
Oak, Samantha	Central Washington University
Oertii, Monica	Central Washington University
Palenshus, Juliet	Central Washington University

Pohl, Amanda	Northern Michigan University
Presnell, Randy	Central Washington University
Ritner, April	Northern Michigan University
Rodriguez, Flavia	Northwestern State University
Roberts, Corey	Tulsa Community College
Rossi, Jessica Ann	Central Washington University
Shafapay, Natasha	Central Washington University
Shanahan, Megan	Northern Michigan University
Teska, Erika	Hawaii Pacific University
Traub, Amy	Northern Michigan University
Underwood, Katie	Central Washington University
Walters, Kim	Central Washington University
Wilson, Kelsie	Central Washington University
Wilson, Amanda	Green River Community College

Series Reviewers

Abraham, Reni	Houston Community College
Agatston, Ann	Agatston Consulting Technical College
Alexander, Melody	Ball Sate University
Alejandro, Manuel	Southwest Texas Junior College
Ali, Farha	Lander University
Amici, Penny	Harrisburg Area Community College
Anderson, Patty A.	Lake City Community College
Andrews, Wilma	Virginia Commonwealth College, Nebraska University
Anik, Mazhar	Tiffin University
Armstrong, Gary	Shippensburg University
Atkins, Bonnie	Delaware Technical Community College
Bachand, LaDonna	Santa Rosa Community College
Bagui, Sikha	University of West Florida
Beecroft, Anita	Kwantlen University College
Bell, Paula	Lock Haven College
Belton, Linda	Springfield Tech. Community College
Bennett, Judith	Sam Houston State University
Bhatia, Sai	Riverside Community College
Bishop, Frances	DeVry Institute—Alpharetta (ATL)
Blaszkiewicz, Holly	Ivy Tech Community College/Region 1
Branigan, Dave	DeVry University
Bray, Patricia	Allegany College of Maryland
Brotherton, Cathy	Riverside Community College
Buehler, Lesley	Ohlone College
Buell, C	Central Oregon Community College
Byars, Pat	Brookhaven College
Byrd, Lynn	Delta State University, Cleveland, Mississippi
Cacace, Richard N.	Pensacola Junior College
Cadenhead, Charles	Brookhaven College
Calhoun, Ric	Gordon College
Cameron, Eric	Passaic Community College
Carriker, Sandra	North Shore Community College
Cannamore, Madie	Kennedy King
Carreon, Cleda	Indiana University—Purdue University, Indianapolis
Chaffin, Catherine	Shawnee State University
Chauvin, Marg	Palm Beach Community College, Boca Raton
Challa, Chandrashekar	Virginia State University
Chamlou, Afsaneh	NOVA Alexandria
Chapman, Pam	Wabaunsee Community College
Christensen, Dan	Iowa Western Community College
Clay, Betty	Southeastern Oklahoma State University
Collins, Linda D.	Mesa Community College
Conroy-Link, Janet	Holy Family College
Cosgrove, Janet	Northwestern CT Community
Courtney, Kevin	Hillsborough Community College
Cox, Rollie	Madison Area Technical College
Crawford, Hiram	Olive Harvey College
Crawford, Thomasina	Miami-Dade College, Kendall Campus
Credico, Grace	Lethbridge Community College
Crenshaw, Richard	Miami Dade Community College, North
Crespo, Beverly	Mt. San Antonio College
Crossley, Connie	Cincinnati State Technical Community College
Curik, Mary	Central New Mexico Community College
De Arazoza, Ralph	Miami Dade Community College
Danno, John	DeVry University/Keller Graduate School
Davis, Phillip	Del Mar College
DeHerrera, Laurie	Pikes Peak Community College
Delk, Dr. K. Kay	Seminole Community College
Doroshow, Mike	Eastfield College
Douglas, Gretchen	SUNYCortland
Dove, Carol	Community College of Allegheny
Driskel, Loretta	Niagara Community College
Duckwiler, Carol	Wabaunsee Community College
Duncan, Mimi	University of Missouri-St. Louis
Duthie, Judy	Green River Community College
Duvall, Annette	Central New Mexico Community College
Ecklund, Paula	Duke University
Eng, Bernice	Brookdale Community College
Evans, Billie	Vance-Granville Community College
Feuerbach, Lisa	Ivy Tech East Chicago
Fisher, Fred	Florida State University
Foster, Penny L.	Anne Arundel Community College
Foszcz, Russ	McHenry County College
Fry, Susan	Boise State University
Fustos, Janos	Metro State
Gallup, Jeanette	Blinn College
Gelb, Janet	Grossmont College
Gentry, Barb	Parkland College
Gerace, Karin	St. Angela Merici School
Gerace, Tom	Tulane University
Ghajar, Homa	Oklahoma State University
Gifford, Steve	Northwest Iowa Community College
Glazer, Ellen	Broward Community College
Gordon, Robert	Hofstra University
Gramlich, Steven	Pasco-Hernando Community College
Graviett, Nancy M.	St. Charles Community College, St. Peters, Missouri
Greene, Rich	Community College of Allegheny County
Gregoryk, Kerry	Virginia Commonwealth State
Griggs, Debra	Bellevue Community College
Grimm, Carol	Palm Beach Community College
Hahn, Norm	Thomas Nelson Community College
Hammerschlag, Dr. Bill	Brookhaven College
Hansen, Michelle	Davenport University
Hayden, Nancy	Indiana University—Purdue University, Indianapolis

Hayes, Theresa	Broward Community College
Helfand, Terri	Chaffey College
Helms, Liz	Columbus State Community College
Hernandez, Leticia	TCI College of Technology
Hibbert, Marilyn	Salt Lake Community College
Hoffman, Joan	Milwaukee Area Technical College
Hogan, Pat	Cape Fear Community College
Holland, Susan	Southeast Community College
Hopson, Bonnie	Athens Technical College
Horvath, Carrie	Albertus Magnus College
Horwitz, Steve	Community College of Philadelphia
Hotta, Barbara	Leeward Community College
Howard, Bunny	St. Johns River Community
Howard, Chris	DeVry University
Huckabay, Jamie	Austin Community College
Hudgins, Susan	East Central University
Hulett, Michelle J.	Missouri State University
Hunt, Darla A.	Morehead State University, Morehead, Kentucky
Hunt, Laura	Tulsa Community College
Jacob, Sherry	Jefferson Community College
Jacobs, Duane	Salt Lake Community College
Jauken, Barb	Southeastern Community
Johnson, Kathy	Wright College
Johnson, Mary	Kingwood College
Johnson, Mary	Mt. San Antonio College
Jones, Stacey	Benedict College
Jones, Warren	University of Alabama, Birmingham
Jordan, Cheryl	San Juan College
Kapoor, Bhushan	California State University, Fullerton
Kasai, Susumu	Salt Lake Community College
Kates, Hazel	Miami Dade Community College, Kendall
Keen, Debby	University of Kentucky
Keeter, Sandy	Seminole Community College
Kern-Blystone, Dorothy Jean	Bowling Green State
Keskin, Ilknur	The University of South Dakota
Kirk, Colleen	Mercy College
Kleckner, Michelle	Elon University
Kliston, Linda	Broward Community College, North Campus
Kochis, Dennis	Suffolk County Community College
Kramer, Ed	Northern Virginia Community College
Laird, Jeff	Northeast State Community College
Lamoureaux, Jackie	Central New Mexico Community College
Lange, David	Grand Valley State
LaPointe, Deb	Central New Mexico Community College
Larson, Donna	Louisville Technical Institute
Laspina, Kathy	Vance-Granville Community College
Le Grand, Dr. Kate	Broward Community College
Lenhart, Sheryl	Terra Community College
Letavec, Chris	University of Cincinnati
Liefert, Jane	Everett Community College
Lindaman, Linda	Black Hawk Community College
Lindberg, Martha	Minnesota State University
Lightner, Renee	Broward Community College
Lindberg, Martha	Minnesota State University
Linge, Richard	Arizona Western College
Logan, Mary G.	Delgado Community College
Loizeaux, Barbara	Westchester Community College
Lopez, Don	Clovis-State Center Community College District
Lord, Alexandria	Asheville Buncombe Tech
Lowe, Rita	Harold Washington College
Low, Willy Hui	Joliet Junior College
Lucas, Vickie	Broward Community College
Lynam, Linda	Central Missouri State University
Lyon, Lynne	Durham College
Lyon, Pat Rajski	Tomball College
MacKinnon, Ruth	Georgia Southern University
Macon, Lisa	Valencia Community College, West Campus
Machuca, Wayne	College of the Sequoias
Madison, Dana	Clarion University
Maguire, Trish	Eastern New Mexico University
Malkan, Rajiv	Montgomery College
Manning, David	Northern Kentucky University
Marcus, Jacquie	Niagara Community College
Marghitu, Daniela	Auburn University
Marks, Suzanne	Bellevue Community College
Marquez, Juanita	El Centro College
Marquez, Juan	Mesa Community College
Martyn, Margie	Baldwin-Wallace College
Marucco, Toni	Lincoln Land Community College
Mason, Lynn	Lubbock Christian University
Matutis, Audrone	Houston Community College
Matkin, Marie	University of Lethbridge
McCain, Evelynn	Boise State University
McCannon, Melinda	Gordon College
McCarthy, Marguerite	Northwestern Business College
McCaskill, Matt L.	Brevard Community College
McClellan, Carolyn	Tidewater Community College
McClure, Darlean	College of Sequoias
McCrory, Sue A.	Missouri State University
McCue, Stacy	Harrisburg Area Community College
McEntire-Orbach, Teresa	Middlesex County College
McLeod, Todd	Fresno City College
McManus, Illyana	Grossmont College
McPherson, Dori	Schoolcraft College
Meiklejohn, Nancy	Pikes Peak Community College
Menking, Rick	Hardin-Simmons University
Meredith, Mary	University of Louisiana at Lafayette
Mermelstein, Lisa	Baruch College
Metos, Linda	Salt Lake Community College
Meurer, Daniel	University of Cincinnati
Meyer, Marian	Central New Mexico Community College
Miller, Cindy	Ivy Tech Community College, Lafayette, Indiana
Mitchell, Susan	Davenport University
Mohle, Dennis	Fresno Community College
Monk, Ellen	University of Delaware
Moore, Rodney	Holland College
Morris, Mike	Southeastern Oklahoma State University
Morris, Nancy	Hudson Valley Community College
Moseler, Dan	Harrisburg Area Community College
Nabors, Brent	Reedley College, Clovis Center
Nadas, Erika	Wright College
Nadelman, Cindi	New England College
Nademlynsky, Lisa	Johnson & Wales University
Ncube, Cathy	University of West Florida
Nagengast, Joseph	Florida Career College
Newsome, Eloise	Northern Virginia Community College Woodbridge
Nicholls, Doreen	Mohawk Valley Community College
Nunan, Karen	Northeast State Technical Community College

Odegard, Teri	Edmonds Community College
Ogle, Gregory	North Community College
Orr, Dr. Claudia	Northern Michigan University South
Otieno, Derek	DeVry University
Otton, Diana Hill	Chesapeake College
Oxendale, Lucia	West Virginia Institute of Technology
Paiano, Frank	Southwestern College
Patrick, Tanya	Clackamas Community College
Peairs, Deb	Clark State Community College
Prince, Lisa	Missouri State University-Springfield Campus
Proietti, Kathleen	Northern Essex Community College
Pusins, Delores	HCCC
Raghuraman, Ram	Joliet Junior College
Reasoner, Ted Allen	Indiana University—Purdue
Reeves, Karen	High Point University
Remillard, Debbie	New Hampshire Technical Institute
Rhue, Shelly	DeVry University
Richards, Karen	Maplewoods Community College
Richardson, Mary	Albany Technical College
Rodgers, Gwen	Southern Nazarene University
Roselli, Diane	Harrisburg Area Community College
Ross, Dianne	University of Louisiana in Lafayette
Rousseau, Mary	Broward Community College, South
Samson, Dolly	Hawaii Pacific University
Sams, Todd	University of Cincinnati
Sandoval, Everett	Reedley College
Sardone, Nancy	Seton Hall University
Scafide, Jean	Mississippi Gulf Coast Community College
Scheeren, Judy	Westmoreland County Community College
Schneider, Sol	Sam Houston State University
Scroggins, Michael	Southwest Missouri State University
Sever, Suzanne	Northwest Arkansas Community College
Sheridan, Rick	California State University-Chico
Silvers, Pamela	Asheville Buncombe Tech
Singer, Steven A.	University of Hawai'i, Kapi'olani Community College
Sinha, Atin	Albany State University
Skolnick, Martin	Florida Atlantic University
Smith, T. Michael	Austin Community College
Smith, Tammy	Tompkins Cortland Community Collge
Smolenski, Bob	Delaware County Community College
Spangler, Candice	Columbus State
Stedham, Vicki	St. Petersburg College, Clearwater
Stefanelli, Greg	Carroll Community College
Steiner, Ester	New Mexico State University
Stenlund, Neal	Northern Virginia Community College, Alexandria
St. John, Steve	Tulsa Community College
Sterling, Janet	Houston Community College
Stoughton, Catherine	Laramie County Community College
Sullivan, Angela	Joliet Junior College
Szurek, Joseph	University of Pittsburgh at Greensburg
Tarver, Mary Beth	Northwestern State University
Taylor, Michael	Seattle Central Community College
Thangiah, Sam	Slippery Rock University
Thompson-Sellers, Ingrid	Georgia Perimeter College
Tomasi, Erik	Baruch College
Toreson, Karen	Shoreline Community College
Trifiletti, John J.	Florida Community College at Jacksonville
Trivedi, Charulata	Quinsigamond Community College, Woodbridge
Tucker, William	Austin Community College
Turgeon, Cheryl	Asnuntuck Community College
Turpen, Linda	Central New Mexico Community College
Upshaw, Susan	Del Mar College
Unruh, Angela	Central Washington University
Vanderhoof, Dr. Glenna	Missouri State University-Springfield Campus
Vargas, Tony	El Paso Community College
Vicars, Mitzi	Hampton University
Villarreal, Kathleen	Fresno
Vitrano, Mary Ellen	Palm Beach Community College
Volker, Bonita	Tidewater Community College
Wahila, Lori (Mindy)	Tompkins Cortland Community College
Waswick, Kim	Southeast Community College, Nebraska
Wavle, Sharon	Tompkins Cortland Community College
Webb, Nancy	City College of San Francisco
Wells, Barbara E.	Central Carolina Technical College
Wells, Lorna	Salt Lake Community College
Welsh, Jean	Lansing Community College Nebraska
White, Bruce	Quinnipiac University
Willer, Ann	Solano Community College
Williams, Mark	Lane Community College
Wilson, Kit	Red River College
Wilson, Roger	Fairmont State University
Wimberly, Leanne	International Academy of Design and Technology
Worthington, Paula	Northern Virginia Community College
Yauney, Annette	Herkimer County Community College
Yip, Thomas	Passaic Community College
Zavala, Ben	Webster Tech
Zlotow, Mary Ann	College of DuPage
Zudeck, Steve	Broward Community College, North

About the Authors

Shelley Gaskin, Series Editor, is a professor of business and computer technology at Pasadena City College in Pasadena, California. She holds a master's degree in business education from Northern Illinois University and a doctorate in adult and community education from Ball State University. Dr. Gaskin has 15 years of experience in the computer industry with several Fortune 500 companies and has developed and written training materials for custom systems applications in both the public and private sector. She is also the author of books on Microsoft Outlook and word processing.

Robert L. Ferrett recently retired as the director of the Center for Instructional Computing at Eastern Michigan University, where he provided computer training and support to faculty. He has authored or co-authored more than 70 books on Access, PowerPoint, Excel, Publisher, WordPerfect, and Word. Before writing for the *GO! Series*, Bob was a series editor and author for the *Learn Series*. He has a bachelor's degree in psychology, a master's degree in geography, and a master's degree in interdisciplinary technology from Eastern Michigan University. Bob's doctoral studies were in instructional technology at Wayne State University. For fun, Bob teaches a four-week computers and genealogy class and has written genealogy and local history books.

John Preston is an Associate Professor at Eastern Michigan University in the College of Technology, where he teaches microcomputer application courses at the undergraduate and graduate levels. He has been teaching, writing, and designing computer training courses since the advent of PCs and has authored and co-authored over 70 books on Microsoft Word, Excel, Access, and PowerPoint. He is a series editor for the Learn 97, Learn 2000, and Learn XP books. Two books on Microsoft Access that he co-authored with Robert Ferrett have been translated into Greek and Chinese. He has received grants from the Detroit Edison Institute and the Department of Energy to develop Web sites for energy education and alternative fuels. He has also developed one of the first Internet-based microcomputer applications courses at an accredited university. He has a bachelor's degree from the University of Michigan in Physics, Mathematics, and Education and a master's degree from Eastern Michigan University in Physics Education. His doctoral studies were in Instructional Technology at Wayne State University.

Sally Preston is president of Preston & Associates, which provides software consulting and training. She currently teaches computing in a variety of settings, which gives her ample opportunity to observe how people learn, what works best, and what challenges are present when learning a new software program. This diverse experience provides a complementary set of skills and knowledge that blends into her writing. Prior to writing for the *GO! Series*, Sally was a co-author on the *Learn* series since its inception and has authored books for the *Essentials* and *Microsoft Office User Specialist (MOUS) Essentials* series. Sally has a master's in business administration from Eastern Michigan University. When away from her computer, she is often found planting flowers in her garden.

Visual Walk-Through of the *GO!* System

The *GO!* System is designed for ease of implementation on the instructor side and ease of understanding on the student. It has been completely developed based on professor and student feedback.

The *GO!* System is divided into three categories that reflect how you might organize your course—**Prepare**, **Teach**, and **Assess**.

Prepare

NEW

Transition Guide

New to *GO!*–We've made it quick and easy to plan the format and activities for your class.

GO!

Because the GO! System was designed and written by instructors like yourself, it includes the tools that allow you to Prepare, Teach, and Assess in your course. We have organized the GO! System into these three categories that match how you work through your course and thus, it's even easier for you to implement.

To help you get started, here is an outline of the first activities you may want to do in order to conduct your course.

There are several other tools not listed here that are available in the GO! System so please refer to your GO! Guide for a complete listing of all the tools.

Prepare
1. Prepare the course syllabus
2. Plan the course assignments
3. Organize the student resources

Teach
4. Conduct demonstrations and lectures

Assess
5. Assign and grade assignments, quizzes, tests, and assessments

PREPARE

1. Prepare the course syllabus
A syllabus template is provided on the IRCD in the **go07_syllabus_template** folder of the main directory. It includes a course calendar planner for 8-week, 12-week, and 16-week formats. Depending on your term (summer or regular semester) you can modify one of these according to your course plan, and then add information pertinent to your course and institution.

2. Plan course assignments
For each chapter, an Assignment Sheet listing every in-chapter and end-of-chapter project is located on the IRCD within the **go01_goloffice2007intro_instructor_resources_by_chapter** folder. From there, navigate to the specific chapter folder. These sheets are Word tables, so you can delete rows for the projects that you choose not to assign or add rows for your own assignments—if any. There is a column to add the number of points you want to assign to each project depending on your grading scheme. At the top of the sheet, you can fill in the course information.

Transitioning to GO! Office 2007 Page 1 of 1

Syllabus Template

Includes course calendar planner for 8-,12-, and 16-week formats.

GO! with Microsoft Office 2007 Introductory
SAMPLE SYLLABUS (16 weeks)

I. COURSE INFORMATION

Course No.: Semester:
Course Title: Credits:
Course Hours:

Instructor: Office:
Office Hours:
Email: Phone:

II. TEXT AND MATERIALS

Before starting the course, you will need the following:

- GO! with Microsoft Office 2007 Introductory by Shelley Gaskin, Robert L. Ferrett, Alicia Vargas, Suzanne Marks ©2007, published by Pearson Prentice Hall.
  ISBN 0-13-167990-6
- Storage device for saving files (any of the following: multiple diskettes, CD-RW, flash drive, etc.)

III. WHAT YOU WILL LEARN IN THIS COURSE

This is a hands-on course where you will learn to use a computer to practice the most commonly used Microsoft programs including the Windows operating system, Internet Explorer for navigating the Internet, Outlook for managing your personal information and the four most popular programs within the Microsoft Office Suite (Word, Excel, PowerPoint and Access). You will also practice the basics of using a computer, mouse and keyboard. You will learn to be an intermediate level user of the Microsoft Office Suite.

Within the Microsoft Office Suite, you will use Word, Excel, PowerPoint, and Access. Microsoft Word is a word processing program with which you can create common business and personal documents. Microsoft Excel is a spreadsheet program that organizes and calculates accounting-type information. Microsoft PowerPoint is a presentation graphics program with which you can develop slides to accompany an oral presentation. Finally, Microsoft Access is a database program that organizes large amounts of information in a useful manner.

Assignment Sheet

One per chapter. Lists all possible assignments; add to and delete from this simple Word table according to your course plan.

GO! with Microsoft Office 2007 Introductory

Assignment Sheet for GO! with Microsoft Office 2007 Introductory
Chapter 5

Instructor Name: ______________________
Course Information: ______________________

Do This (✓ when done)	Then Hand in This Check each Project for the elements listed on the Assignment Tag. Attach the Tag to your Project.	Submit Printed Formulas	By This Date	Possible Points	Your Points
Study the text and perform the steps for Activities 5.1 – 5.11	Project 5A Application Letter				
Study the text and perform the steps for Activities 5.12 – 5.23	Project 5B Company Overview				
End-of-Chapter Assessments					
Complete the Matching and Fill-in-the-Blank questions	As directed by your instructor				
Complete Project 5C	Project 5C Receipt Letter				
Complete Project 5D	Project 5D Marketing				
Complete Project 5E	Project 5E School Tour				
Complete Project 5F	Project 5F Scouting Trip				
Complete Project 5G	Project 5G Contract				
Complete Project 5H	Project 5H Invitation				
Complete Project 5I	Project 5I Fax Cover				
Complete Project 5J	Project 5J Business Running Case				
Complete Project 5K	Project 5K Services				
Complete Project 5L	Project 5L Survey Form				
Complete Project 5M	Project 5M Press Release				

Copyright © 2008 Pearson Prentice Hall — Page 1 of 1

File Guide to the *GO!* Supplements

Tabular listing of all supplements and their file names.

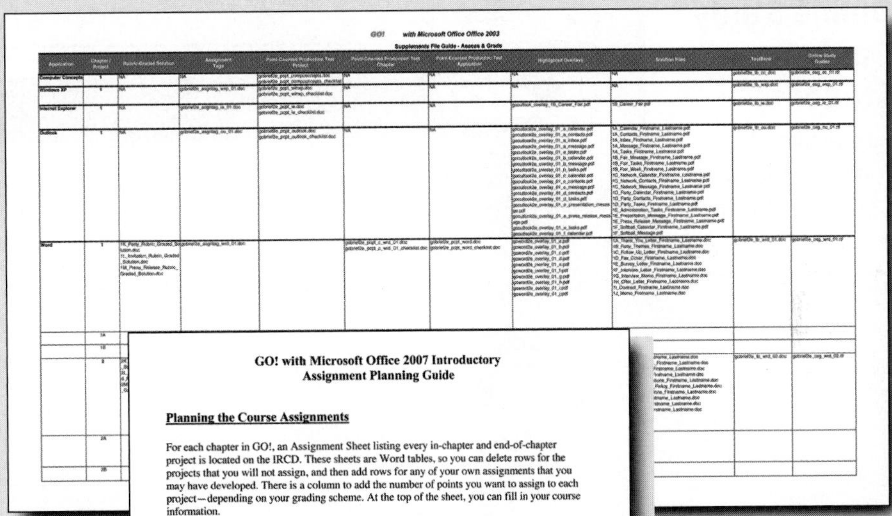

GO! with Microsoft Office Office 2003
Supplements File Guide - Assets & Grade

NEW

Assignment Planning Guide

Description of *GO!* assignments with recommendations based on class size, delivery mode, and student needs. Includes examples from fellow instructors.

GO! with Microsoft Office 2007 Introductory
Assignment Planning Guide

Planning the Course Assignments

For each chapter in GO!, an Assignment Sheet listing every in-chapter and end-of-chapter project is located on the IRCD. These sheets are Word tables, so you can delete rows for the projects that you will not assign, and then add rows for any of your own assignments that you may have developed. There is a column to add the number of points you want to assign to each project—depending on your grading scheme. At the top of the sheet, you can fill in your course information.

Additionally, for each chapter, student Assignment Tags are provided for every project (including Problem Solving projects)—also located on the IRCD. These are small scoring checklists on which you can check off errors made by the student, and with which the student can verify that all project elements are complete. For campus classes, the student can attach the tags to his or her paper submissions. For online classes, many GO! instructors have the student include these with the electronic submission.

Deciding What to Assign

Front Portion of the Chapter—Instructional Projects: The projects in the front portion of the chapter, which are listed on the first page of each chapter, are the instructional projects. Most instructors assign all of these projects, because this is where the student receives the instruction and engages in the active learning.

End-of-Chapter—Practice and Critical Thinking Projects: In the back portion of the chapter (the gray pages), you can assign on a prescriptive basis; that is, for students who were challenged by the instructional projects, you might assign one or more projects from the two *Skills Reviews*, which provide maximum prompting and a thorough review of the entire chapter. For students who have previous software knowledge and who completed the instructional projects easily, you might assign only the *Mastery Projects*.

You can also assign prescriptively by Objective, because each end-of-chapter project indicates the Objectives covered. So you might assign, on a student-by-student basis, only the projects that cover the Objectives with which the student seemed to have difficulty in the instructional projects.

The five Problem Solving projects and the You and GO! project are the authentic assessments that pull together the student's learning. Here the student is presented with a "messy real-life situation" and then uses his or her knowledge and skill to solve a problem, produce a product, give a presentation, or demonstrate a procedure. You might assign one or more of the Problem

GO! Assignment Planning Guide — Page 1 of 1

Student Data Files

Music School Records discovers, launches, and and develops the careers of young artists in classical, jazz, and contemporary music. Our philosophy is to not only shape, distribute, and sell a music product, but to help artists create a career that can lats a lifetime. too often in the music industry, artists are forced to fit their music to a trend that is short-lived. Music School Records doesn't just follow trends, we take a long-term view of the music industry and help our artists develop a style and repertiore that is fluid and flexible and that will appeal to audiences for years and even decades.

The music industry is constantly changing, but over the last decade the changes have been enormous. New forms of entertainment such as DVDs, video games, and the Internet mean there are more competition for the leisure dollar in the market. New technologies give consumers more options for buying and listening to music, and they are demaning high quality recordings. Young consumers are comfortable with technology and want the music they love when and where they want it, no matter where they are or what they are doing.

Music School Records embraces new technologies and the sophisticated market of young music lovers. We believe that providing high quality recordings of truly talented artists make for more discerning listeners who will cherish the gift of music for the rest of their lives. The expertise of Music School Records includes:

- Insight into our target market and the ability to reach the desired audience
- The ability to access all current sources of music income
- A management team with years of experience in music commerce
- Innovative business strategies and artist development plans
- Investment in technology infrastructure for high quality recordings and business services
- Initiative and proactive management of artist careers

Online Study Guide for Students

Interactive objective-style questions based on chapter content.

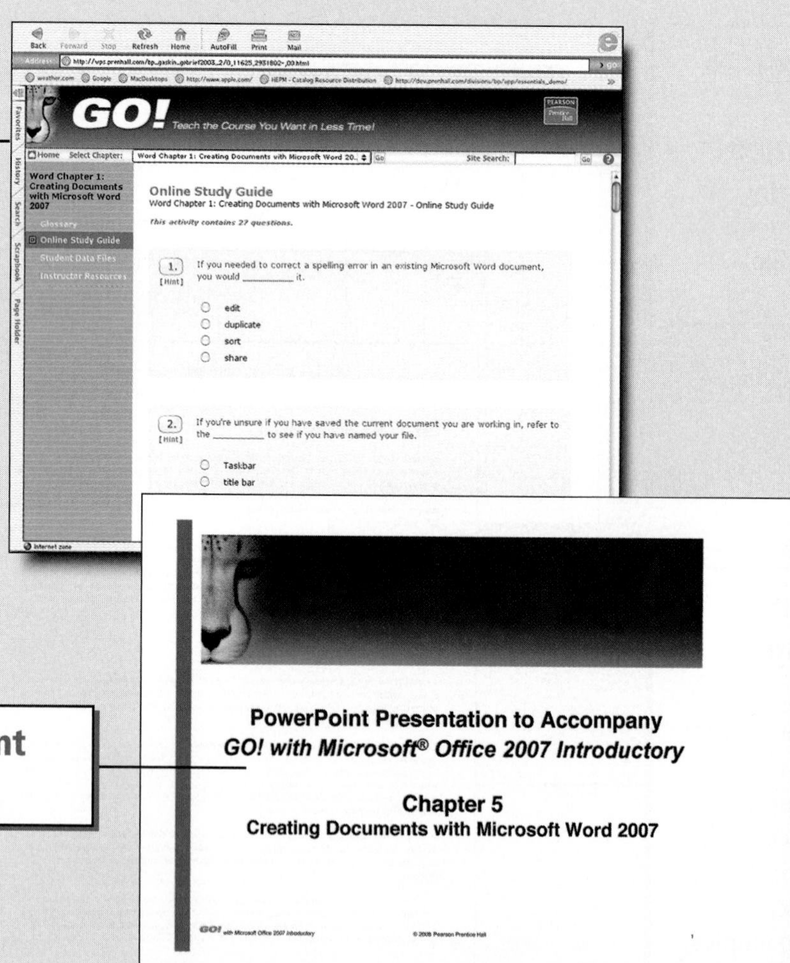

PowerPoint Slides

Teach

Student Textbook

Learning Objectives and Student Outcomes

Objectives are clustered around projects that result in student outcomes. They help students learn how to solve problems, not just learn software features.

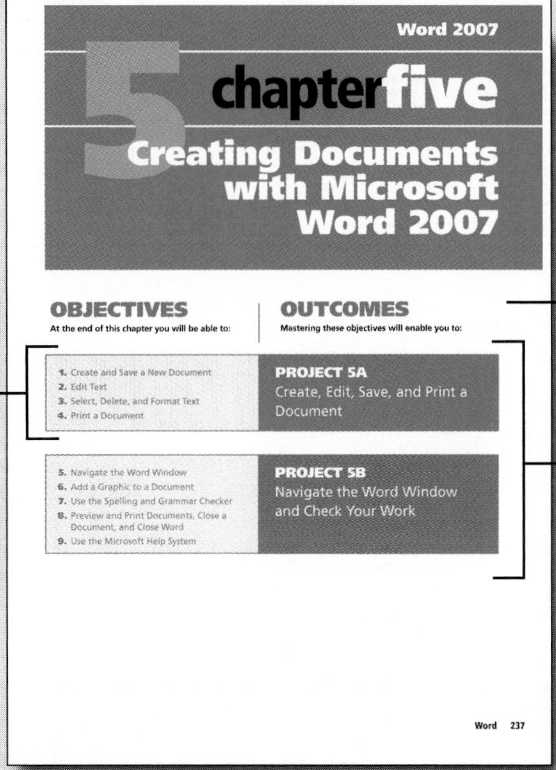

Word 2007

5 chapterfive

Creating Documents with Microsoft Word 2007

OBJECTIVES
At the end of this chapter you will be able to:

OUTCOMES
Mastering these objectives will enable you to:

1. Create and Save a New Document
2. Edit Text
3. Select, Delete, and Format Text
4. Print a Document

PROJECT 5A
Create, Edit, Save, and Print a Document

5. Navigate the Word Window
6. Add a Graphic to a Document
7. Use the Spelling and Grammar Checker
8. Preview and Print Documents, Close a Document, and Close Word
9. Use the Microsoft Help System

PROJECT 5B
Navigate the Word Window and Check Your Work

Word 237

Project-Based Instruction

Students do not practice features of the application; they create real projects that they will need in the real world. Projects are color coded for easy reference and are named to reflect skills the students will be practicing.

NEW

A and B Projects

Each chapter contains two instructional projects—A and B.

Music School Records

Music School Records was created to launch young musical artists with undiscovered talent in jazz, classical, and contemporary music. The creative management team searches internationally for talented young people, and has a reputation for mentoring and developing the skills of its artists. The company's music is tailored to an audience that is young, knowledgeable about music, and demands the highest quality recordings. Music School Records releases are available in CD format as well as digital downloads.

Getting Started with Microsoft Office Word 2007

A word processor is the most common program found on personal computers and one that almost everyone has a reason to use. When you learn word processing you are also learning skills and techniques that you need to work efficiently on a personal computer. You can use Microsoft Word to perform basic word processing tasks such as writing a memo, a report, or a letter. You can also use Word to complete complex word processing tasks, such as those that include sophisticated tables, embedded graphics, and links to other documents and the Internet. Word is a program that you can learn gradually, and then add more advanced skills one at a time.

Each chapter opens with a story that sets the stage for the projects the student will create; the instruction does not force the student to pretend to be someone or make up a scenario.

Each chapter has an introductory paragraph that briefs students on what is important.

Teach (continued)

Visual Summary
Shows students upfront what their projects will look like when they are done.

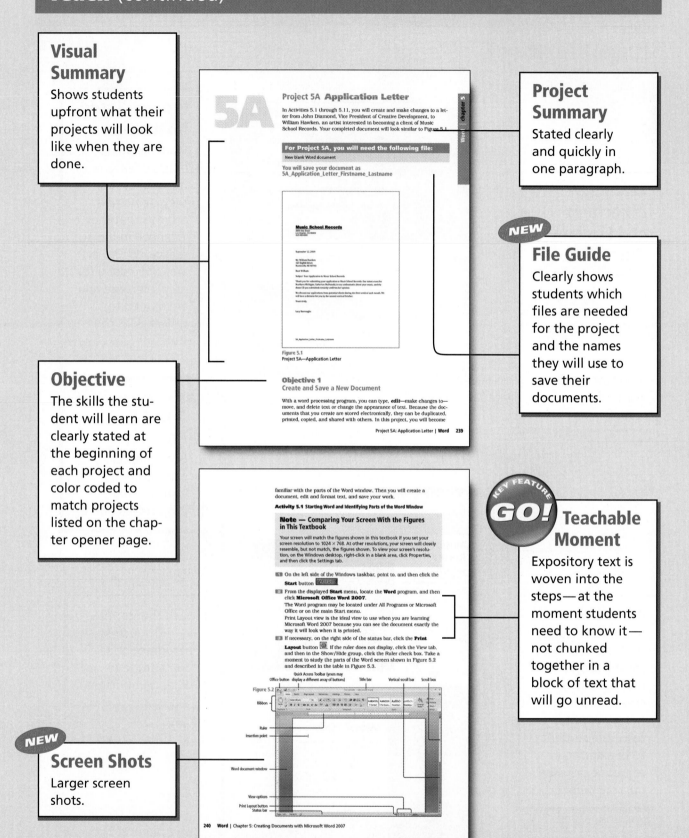

Project Summary
Stated clearly and quickly in one paragraph.

NEW

File Guide
Clearly shows students which files are needed for the project and the names they will use to save their documents.

Objective
The skills the student will learn are clearly stated at the beginning of each project and color coded to match projects listed on the chapter opener page.

5A

Project 5A **Application Letter**

In Activities 5.1 through 5.11, you will create and make changes to a letter from John Diamond, Vice President of Creative Development, to William Hawken, an artist interested in becoming a client of Music School Records. Your completed document will look similar to Figure 5.1.

Word | chapter 5

For Project 5A, you will need the following file:

New blank Word document

You will save your document as
5A_Application_Letter_Firstname_Lastname

Music School Records

Figure 5.1
Project 5A—Application Letter

Objective 1
Create and Save a New Document

With a word processing program, you can type, *edit*—make changes to—move, and delete text or change the appearance of text. Because the documents that you create are stored electronically, they can be duplicated, printed, copied, and shared with others. In this project, you will become

Project 5A: Application Letter | **Word** 239

KEY FEATURE GO!

Teachable Moment
Expository text is woven into the steps—at the moment students need to know it—not chunked together in a block of text that will go unread.

familiar with the parts of the Word window. Then you will create a document, edit and format text, and save your work.

Activity 5.1 Starting Word and Identifying Parts of the Word Window

Note — Comparing Your Screen With the Figures in This Textbook

Your screen will match the figures shown in this textbook if you set your screen resolution to 1024 × 768. At other resolutions, your screen will closely resemble, but not match, the figures shown. To view your screen's resolution, on the Windows desktop, right-click in a blank area, click Properties, and then click the Settings tab.

1. On the left side of the Windows taskbar, point to, and then click the **Start** button.
2. From the displayed **Start** menu, locate the **Word** program, and then click **Microsoft Office Word 2007**.
   The Word program may be located under All Programs or Microsoft Office or on the main Start menu.
   Print Layout view is the ideal view to use when you are learning Microsoft Word 2007 because you can see the document exactly the way it will look when it is printed.
3. If necessary, on the right side of the status bar, click the **Print Layout** button. If the ruler does not display, click the View tab, and then in the Show/Hide group, click the Ruler check box. Take a moment to study the parts of the Word screen shown in Figure 5.2 and described in the table in Figure 5.3.

Figure 5.2

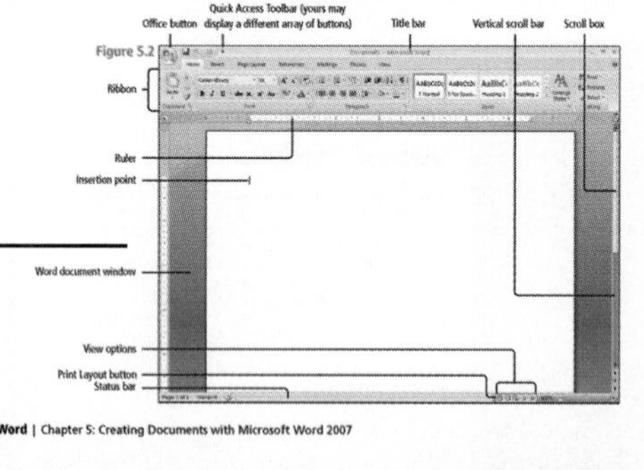

240 **Word** | Chapter 5: Creating Documents with Microsoft Word 2007

NEW

Screen Shots
Larger screen shots.

Steps
Color coded to the current project, easy to read, and not too many to confuse the student or too few to be meaningless.

KEY FEATURE GO! Sequential Pagination
No more confusing letters and abbreviations.

KEY FEATURE GO! Microsoft Procedural Syntax
All steps are written in Microsoft Procedural Syntax to put the student in the right place at the right time.

5 Press Enter two more times.

In a business letter, insert two blank lines between the date and the inside address, which is the same as the address you would use on an envelope.

6 Type **Mr. William Hawken** and then press Enter.

The wavy red line under the proper name *Hawken* indicates that the word has been flagged as misspelled because it is a word not contained in the Word dictionary.

7 On two lines, type the following address, but do not press Enter at the end of the second line:

123 Eighth Street
Harrisville, MI 48740

Note — Typing the Address

Include a comma after the city name in an inside address. However, for mailing addresses on envelopes, eliminate the comma after the city name.

8 On the **Home tab**, in the **Styles group**, click the **Normal** button.

The Normal style is applied to the text in the rest of the document. Recall that the Normal style adds extra space between paragraphs; it also adds slightly more space between lines in a paragraph.

9 Press Enter. Type **Dear William:** and then press Enter.

This salutation is the line that greets the person receiving the letter.

10 Type **Subject: Your Application to Music School Records** and press Enter. Notice the light dots between words, which indicate spaces and display when formatting marks are displayed. Also, notice the extra space after each paragraph, and then compare your screen with Figure 5.6.

The subject line is optional, but you should include a subject line in most letters to identify the topic. Depending on your Word settings, a wavy green line may display in the subject line, indicating a potential grammar error.

244 **Word** | Chapter 5: Creating Documents with Microsoft Word 2007

End-of-Project Icon
All projects in the *GO! Series* have clearly identifiable end points, useful in self-paced or online environments.

Note — Space Between Lines in Your Printed Document

The Cambria font, and many others, uses a slightly larger space between the lines than more traditional fonts like Times New Roman. As you progress in your study of Word, you will use many different fonts and also adjust the spacing between lines.

3 From the **Office** menu, click **Close**, saving any changes if prompted to do so. Leave Word open for the next project.

Another Way

To Print a Document

To Print a document:

- From the Office menu, click Print to display the Print dialog box (to be covered later), from which you can choose a variety of different options, such as printing multiple copies, printing on a different printer, and printing some but not all pages.
- Hold down Ctrl and then press P. This is an alternative to the Office menu command, and opens the Print dialog box.
- Hold down Alt, press F, and then press P. This opens the Print dialog box.

End **You have completed Project 5A**

264 **Word** | Chapter 5: Creating Documents with Microsoft Word 2007

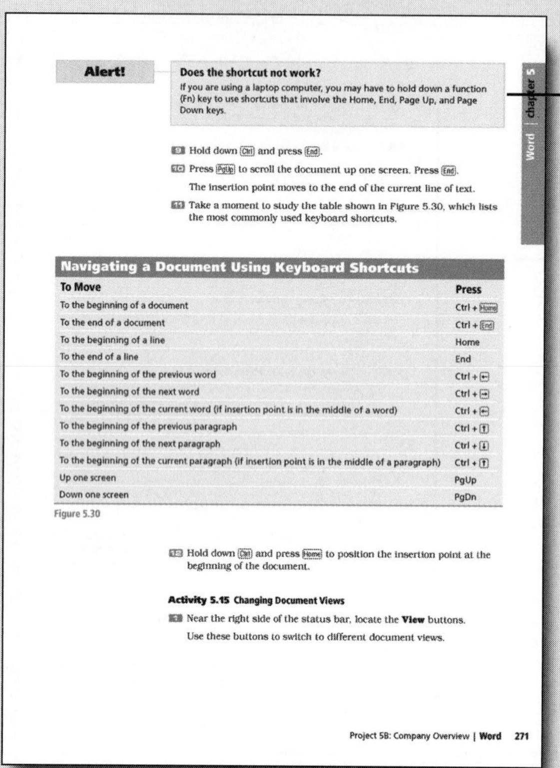

Alert!

Does the shortcut not work?
If you are using a laptop computer, you may have to hold down a function (Fn) key to use shortcuts that involve the Home, End, Page Up, and Page Down keys.

9 Hold down Ctrl and press End.

10 Press PgUp to scroll the document up one screen. Press End.

The insertion point moves to the end of the current line of text.

11 Take a moment to study the table shown in Figure 5.30, which lists the most commonly used keyboard shortcuts.

Navigating a Document Using Keyboard Shortcuts

To Move	Press
To the beginning of a document	Ctrl + Home
To the end of a document	Ctrl + End
To the beginning of a line	Home
To the end of a line	End
To the beginning of the previous word	Ctrl + ←
To the beginning of the next word	Ctrl + →
To the beginning of the current word (if insertion point is in the middle of a word)	Ctrl + ←
To the beginning of the previous paragraph	Ctrl + ↑
To the beginning of the next paragraph	Ctrl + ↓
To the beginning of the current paragraph (if insertion point is in the middle of a paragraph)	Ctrl + ↑
Up one screen	PgUp
Down one screen	PgDn

Figure 5.30

12 Hold down Ctrl and press Home to position the insertion point at the beginning of the document.

Activity 5.15 Changing Document Views

1 Near the right side of the status bar, locate the **View** buttons.

Use these buttons to switch to different document views.

Word | chapter 5

Project 5B: Company Overview | **Word** 271

Alert box

Draws students' attention to make sure they aren't getting too far off course.

Another Way box

Shows students other ways of doing tasks.

More Knowledge box

Expands on a topic by going deeper into the material.

Note box

Points out important items to remember.

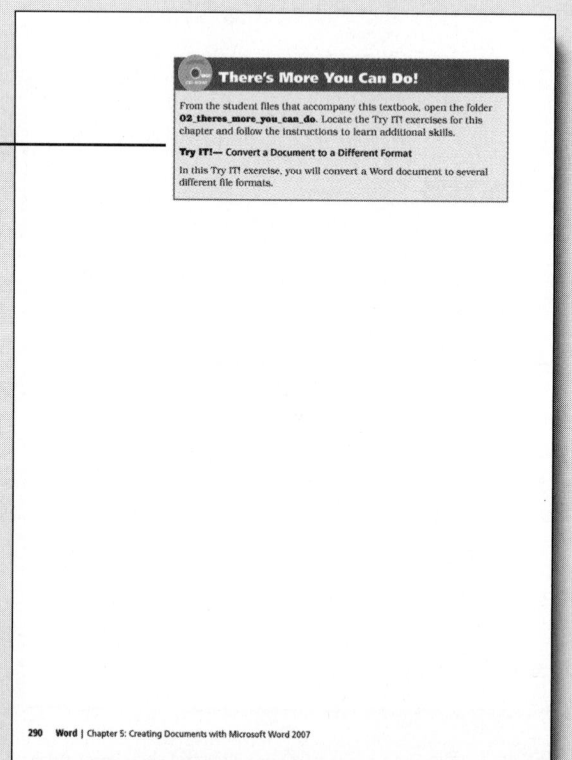

There's More You Can Do!

From the student files that accompany this textbook, open the folder **02_theres_more_you_can_do**. Locate the Try IT! exercises for this chapter and follow the instructions to learn additional skills.

Try IT!— Convert a Document to a Different Format

In this Try IT! exercise, you will convert a Word document to several different file formats.

290 **Word** | Chapter 5: Creating Documents with Microsoft Word 2007

NEW

There's More You Can Do!

Try IT! exercises that teach students additional skills.

End-of-Chapter Material

Take your pick! Content-based or Outcomes-based projects to choose from. Below is a table outlining the various types of projects that fit into these two categories.

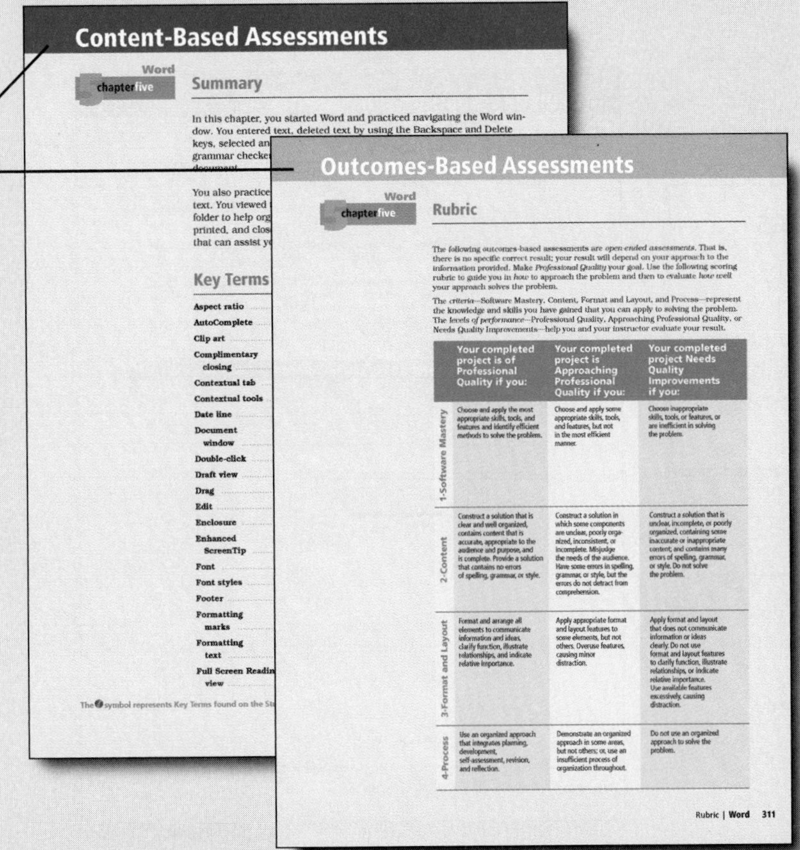

Content-Based Assessments

Word chapter five

Summary

In this chapter, you started Word and practiced navigating the Word window. You entered text, deleted text by using the Backspace and Delete keys, selected an

Key Terms

Aspect ratio
AutoComplete
Clip art
Complimentary closing
Contextual tab
Contextual tools
Date line
Document window
Double-click
Draft view
Drag
Edit
Enclosure
Enhanced ScreenTip
Font
Font styles
Footer
Formatting marks
Formatting text
Full Screen Reading view

Outcomes-Based Assessments

Word chapter five

Rubric

The following outcomes-based assessments are *open-ended assessments*. That is, there is no specific correct result; your result will depend on your approach to the information provided. Make *Professional Quality* your goal. Use the following scoring rubric to guide you in *how* to approach the problem and then to evaluate *how well* your approach solves the problem.

The *criteria*—Software Mastery, Content, Format and Layout, and Process—represent the knowledge and skills you have gained that you can apply to solving the problem. The *levels of performance*—Professional Quality, Approaching Professional Quality, or Needs Quality Improvements—help you and your instructor evaluate your result.

	Your completed project is of Professional Quality if you:	Your completed project is Approaching Professional Quality if you:	Your completed project Needs Quality Improvements if you:
1-Software Mastery	Choose and apply the most appropriate skills, tools, and features and identify efficient methods to solve the problem.	Choose and apply some appropriate skills, tools, and features, but not in the most efficient manner.	Choose inappropriate skills, tools, or features, or are inefficient in solving the problem.
2-Content	Construct a solution that is clear and well organized, contains content that is accurate, appropriate to the audience and purpose, and is complete. Provide a solution that contains no errors of spelling, grammar, or style.	Construct a solution in which some components are unclear, poorly organized, inconsistent, or incomplete. Misjudge the needs of the audience. Have some errors in spelling, grammar, or style, but the errors do not detract from comprehension.	Construct a solution that is unclear, incomplete, or poorly organized, containing some inaccurate or inappropriate content; and contains many errors of spelling, grammar, or style. Do not solve the problem.
3-Format and Layout	Format and arrange all elements to communicate information and ideas, clarify function, illustrate relationships, and indicate relative importance.	Apply appropriate format and layout features to some elements, but not others. Overuse features, causing minor distraction.	Apply format and layout that does not communicate information or ideas clearly. Do not use format and layout features to clarify function, illustrate relationships, or indicate relative importance. Use available features excessively, causing distraction.
4-Process	Use an organized approach that integrates planning, development, self-assessment, revision, and reflection.	Demonstrate an organized approach in some areas, but not others; or, use an insufficient process of organization throughout.	Do not use an organized approach to solve the problem.

Rubric | Word 311

Content-Based Assessments

(Defined solutions with solution files provided for grading)

Project Letter	Name	Objectives Covered
N/A	Summary and Key Terms	
N/A	Multiple Choice	
N/A	Fill-in-the-blank	
C	Skills Review	Covers A Objectives
D	Skills Review	Covers B Objectives
E	Mastering Excel	Covers A Objectives
F	Mastering Excel	Covers B Objectives
G	Mastering Excel	Covers any combination of A and B Objectives
H	Mastering Excel	Covers any combination of A and B Objectives
I	Mastering Excel	Covers all A and B Objectives
J	Business Running Case	Covers all A and B Objectives

Outcomes-Based Assessments

(Open solutions that require a rubric for grading)

Project Letter	Name	Objectives Covered
N/A	Rubric	
K	Problem Solving	Covers as many Objectives from A and B as possible
L	Problem Solving	Covers as many Objectives from A and B as possible.
M	Problem Solving	Covers as many Objectives from A and B as possible.
N	Problem Solving	Covers as many Objectives from A and B as possible.
O	Problem Solving	Covers as many Objectives from A and B as possible.
P	You and GO!	Covers as many Objectives from A and B as possible
Q	GO! Help	Not tied to specific objectives
R	* Group Business Running Case	Covers A and B Objectives

* This project is provided only with the *GO! with Microsoft Office 2007 Introductory* book.

Objectives List

Most projects in the end-of-chapter section begin with a list of the objectives covered.

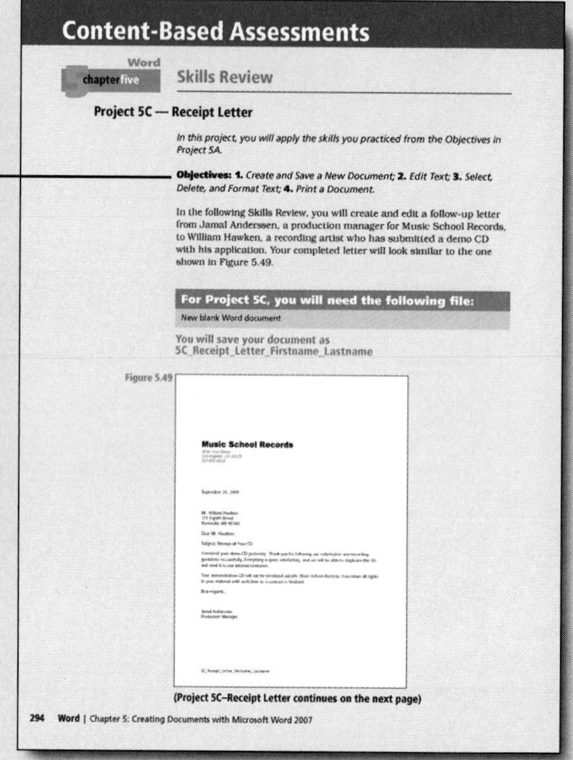

Content-Based Assessments

Word chapter five — Skills Review

Project 5C — Receipt Letter

In this project, you will apply the skills you practiced from the Objectives in Project 5A.

Objectives: **1.** *Create and Save a New Document;* **2.** *Edit Text;* **3.** *Select, Delete, and Format Text;* **4.** *Print a Document.*

In the following Skills Review, you will create and edit a follow-up letter from Jamal Anderssen, a production manager for Music School Records, to William Hawken, a recording artist who has submitted a demo CD with his application. Your completed letter will look similar to the one shown in Figure 5.49.

For Project 5C, you will need the following file:

New blank Word document

You will save your document as
5C_Receipt_Letter_Firstname_Lastname

Figure 5.49

Music School Records

(Project 5C–Receipt Letter continues on the next page)

294 Word | Chapter 5: Creating Documents with Microsoft Word 2007

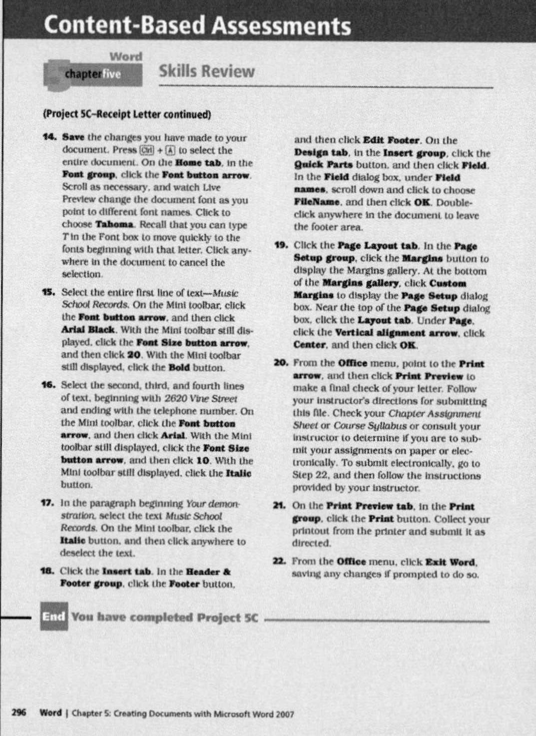

Content-Based Assessments

Word chapter five — Skills Review

(Project 5C–Receipt Letter continued)

14. **Save** the changes you have made to your document. Press Ctrl + A to select the entire document. On the **Home tab**, in the **Font group**, click the **Font button arrow**. Scroll as necessary, and watch Live Preview change the document font as you point to different font names. Click to choose **Tahoma**. Recall that you can type *T* in the Font box to move quickly to the fonts beginning with that letter. Click anywhere in the document to cancel the selection.

15. Select the entire first line of text—*Music School Records*. On the Mini toolbar, click the **Font button arrow**, and then click **Arial Black**. With the Mini toolbar still displayed, click the **Font Size button arrow**, and then click **20**. With the Mini toolbar still displayed, click the **Bold** button.

16. Select the second, third, and fourth lines of text, beginning with *2620 Vine Street* and ending with the telephone number. On the Mini toolbar, click the **Font button arrow**, and then click **Arial**. With the Mini toolbar still displayed, click the **Font Size button arrow**, and then click **10**. With the Mini toolbar still displayed, click the **Italic** button.

17. In the paragraph beginning *Your demonstration*, select the text *Music School Records*. On the Mini toolbar, click the **Italic** button, and then click anywhere to deselect the text.

18. Click the **Insert tab**. In the **Header & Footer group**, click the **Footer** button, and then click **Edit Footer**. On the **Design tab**, in the **Insert group**, click the **Quick Parts** button, and then click **Field**. In the **Field** dialog box, under **Field names**, scroll down and click to choose **FileName**, and then click **OK**. Double-click anywhere in the document to leave the footer area.

19. Click the **Page Layout tab**. In the **Page Setup group**, click the **Margins** button to display the Margins gallery. At the bottom of the **Margins gallery**, click **Custom Margins** to display the **Page Setup** dialog box. Near the top of the **Page Setup** dialog box, click the **Layout tab**. Under **Page**, click the **Vertical alignment arrow**, click **Center**, and then click **OK**.

20. From the **Office** menu, point to the **Print arrow**, and then click **Print Preview** to make a final check of your letter. Follow your instructor's directions for submitting this file. Check your *Chapter Assignment Sheet* or *Course Syllabus* or consult your instructor to determine if you are to submit your assignments on paper or electronically. To submit electronically, go to Step 22, and then follow the instructions provided by your instructor.

21. On the **Print Preview tab**, in the **Print group**, click the **Print** button. Collect your printout from the printer and submit it as directed.

22. From the **Office** menu, click **Exit Word**, saving any changes if prompted to do so.

End **You have completed Project 5C**

296 Word | Chapter 5: Creating Documents with Microsoft Word 2007

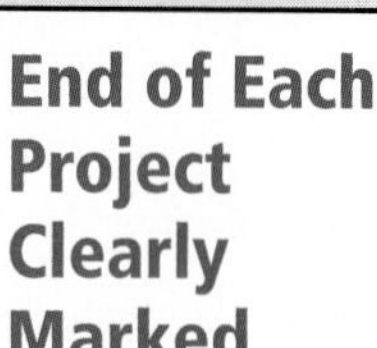

End of Each Project Clearly Marked

Clearly identified end points help separate the end-of-chapter projects.

NEW

Rubric

A matrix that states the criteria and standards for grading student work. Used to grade open-ended assessments.

Outcomes-Based Assessments

Word
chapter five

Rubric

The following outcomes-based assessments are *open-ended assessments*. That is, there is no specific correct result; your result will depend on your approach to the information provided. Make *Professional Quality* your goal. Use the following scoring rubric to guide you in *how* to approach the problem and then to evaluate *how well* your approach solves the problem.

The *criteria*—Software Mastery, Content, Format and Layout, and Process—represent the knowledge and skills you have gained that you can apply to solving the problem. The *levels of performance*—Professional Quality, Approaching Professional Quality, or Needs Quality Improvements—help you and your instructor evaluate your result.

	Your completed project is of Professional Quality if you:	Your completed project is Approaching Professional Quality if you:	Your completed project Needs Quality Improvements if you:
1-Software Mastery	Choose and apply the most appropriate skills, tools, and features and identify efficient methods to solve the problem.	Choose and apply some appropriate skills, tools, and features, but not in the most efficient manner.	Choose inappropriate skills, tools, or features, or are inefficient in solving the problem.
2-Content	Construct a solution that is clear and well organized, contains content that is accurate, appropriate to the audience and purpose, and is complete. Provide a solution that contains no errors of spelling, grammar, or style.	Construct a solution in which some components are unclear, poorly organized, inconsistent, or incomplete. Misjudge the needs of the audience. Have some errors in spelling, grammar, or style, but the errors do not detract from comprehension.	Construct a solution that is unclear, incomplete, or poorly organized, containing some inaccurate or inappropriate content; and contains many errors of spelling, grammar, or style. Do not solve the problem.
3-Format and Layout	Format and arrange all elements to communicate information and ideas, clarify function, illustrate relationships, and indicate relative importance.	Apply appropriate format and layout features to some elements, but not others. Overuse features, causing minor distraction.	Apply format and layout that does not communicate information or ideas clearly. Do not use format and layout features to clarify function, illustrate relationships, or indicate relative importance. Use available features excessively, causing distraction.
4-Process	Use an organized approach that integrates planning, development, self-assessment, revision, and reflection.	Demonstrate an organized approach in some areas, but not others; or, use an insufficient process of organization throughout.	Do not use an organized approach to solve the problem.

Rubric | **Word** 311

Outcomes-Based Assessments

Word
chapter five

You and *GO!*

NEW

You and *GO!*

A project in which students use information from their own lives and apply the skills from the chapter to a personal task.

Project 5P—You and *Go!*

In this project, you will construct a solution by applying any combination of the skills you practiced from the Objectives in Projects 5A and 5B.

From the student files that accompany this textbook, open the folder **04_you_and_go**. Locate the You and *GO!* project for this chapter and follow the instructions to create a cover letter for your resume.

End **You have completed Project 5P**

GO! with Help

Students practice using the Help feature of the Office application.

GO! with Help

Project 5Q—*Go!* with Help

The Word Help system is extensive and can help you as you work. In this chapter, you used the Quick Access Toolbar on several occasions. You can customize the Quick Access Toolbar by adding buttons that you use regularly, making them quickly available to you from any tab on the Ribbon. In this project, you will use Help to find out how to add buttons.

1. **Start** Word. At the far right end of the Ribbon, click the **Microsoft Office Word Help** button. In the **Word Help** dialog box, click the **Search button arrow**, and then click **Offline Word Help**.
2. In the **Type words to search for** box, type **Quick Access Toolbar** and then press Enter.
3. From the list of search results, click **Customize the Quick Access Toolbar**.
4. Click each of the links to find out how to add buttons from the Ribbon and from the **Options** dialog box.
5. When you are through, **Close** the Help window, and then **Close** Word.

End **You have completed Project 5Q**

318 **Word** | Chapter 5: Creating Documents with Microsoft Word 2007

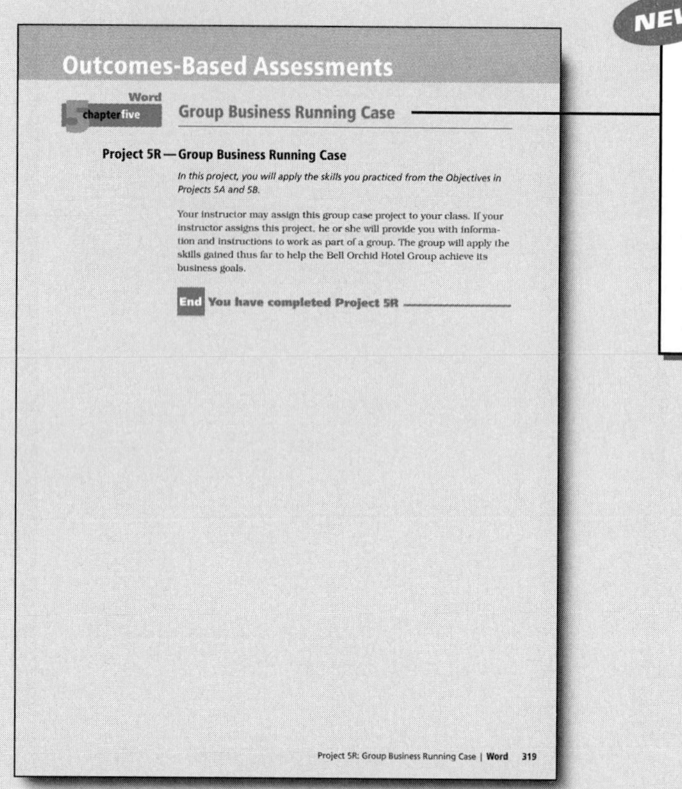

NEW

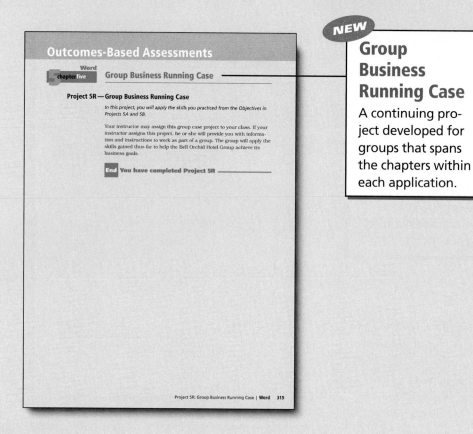

Group Business Running Case

A continuing project developed for groups that spans the chapters within each application.

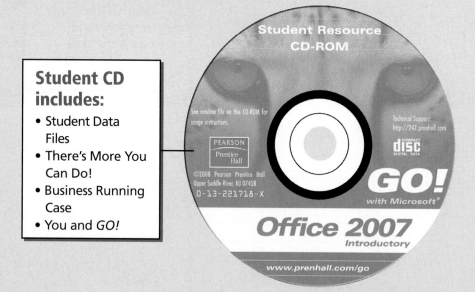

Student CD includes:

- Student Data Files
- There's More You Can Do!
- Business Running Case
- You and *GO!*

Companion Web site

An interactive Web site to further student leaning.

Online Study Guide

Interactive objective-style questions to help students study.

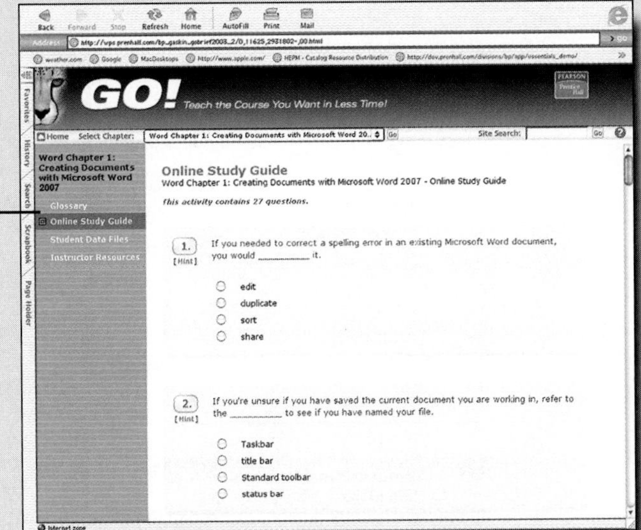

Teach (continued)

Annotated Instructor Edition

The Annotated Instructor Edition contains a full version of the student textbook that includes tips, supplement references, and pointers on teaching with the *GO!* instructional system.

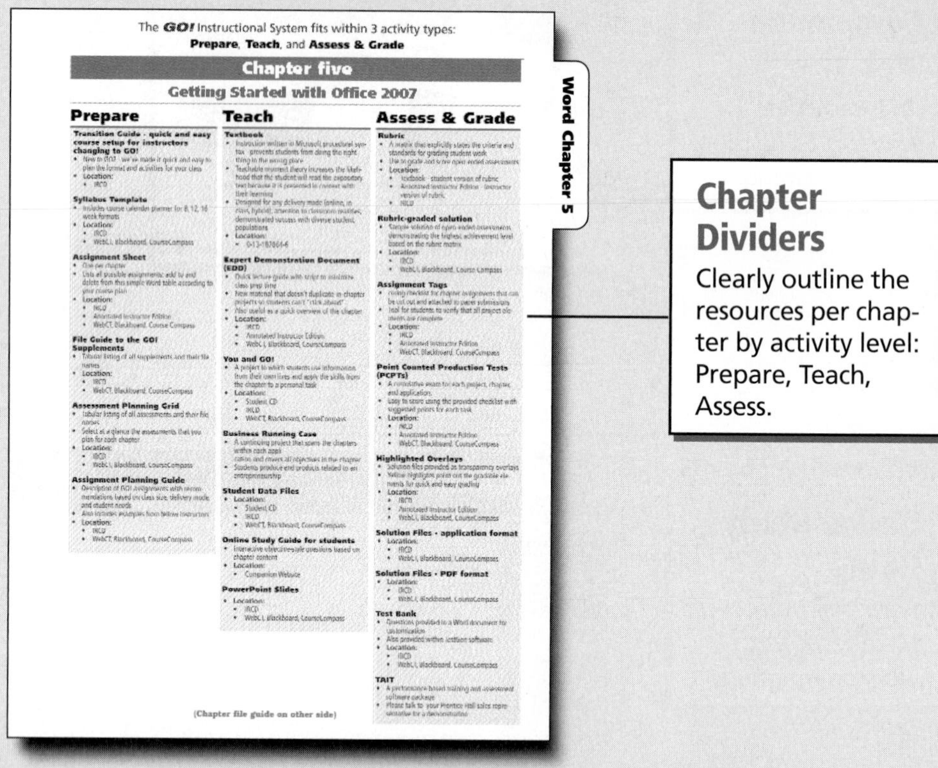

The *GO!* Instructional System fits within 3 activity types:
Prepare, **Teach**, and **Assess & Grade**

Word Chapter 5

Chapter five

Getting Started with Office 2007

Prepare

- **Transition Guide - quick and easy course setup for instructors changing to GO!**
- **Syllabus Template**
- **Assignment Sheet**
- **File Guide to the GO! Supplements**
- **Assessment Planning Grid**
- **Assignment Planning Guide**

Teach

- **Textbook**
- **Expert Demonstration Document (EDD)**
- **You and GO!**
- **Business Running Case**
- **Student Data Files**
- **Online Study Guide for students**
- **PowerPoint Slides**

Assess & Grade

- **Rubric**
- **Rubric-graded solution**
- **Assignment Tags**
- **Point Counted Production Tests (PCPTs)**
- **Highlighted Overlays**
- **Solution Files - application format**
- **Solution Files - PDF format**
- **Test Bank**
- **TAIT**

(Chapter file guide on other side)

Chapter Dividers
Clearly outline the resources per chapter by activity level: Prepare, Teach, Assess.

Chapter Five File Guide

Getting Started with Office 2007

Project	Student Data Files	Teacher Solution Files
1A	Blank Word document	1A_Thank_You_Letter_Firstname_Lastname
1B	w01B_Party_Themes w01B_Perfect_Party_Logo	1B_Party_Themes_Firstname_Lastname
1C	Blank Word document w01C_Follow_Up_Letter	1C_Follow_Up_Letter_Firstname_Lastname
1D	Blank Word document w01D_Fax_Machine	1D_Fax_Cover_Firstname_Lastname
1E	w01E_Survey_Letter	1D_Survey_Letter_Firstname_Lastname
1F	Blank Word document	1F_Interview_Letter_Firstname_Lastname
1G	w01G_Interview_Memo	1G_Interview_Memo_Firstname_Lastname
1H	w01H_Offer_Letter w01H_Caterer	1H_Offer_Letter_Firstname_Lastname
1I	w01I_Contract	1I_Contract_Firstname_Lastname
1J	Blank Word document w01J_Memo	1J_Memo_Firstname_Lastname
1K	Blank Word document	1K_Party_Firstname_Lastname
1L	Blank Word document	1L_Invitation_Firstname_Lastname
1M	Blank Word document w01M_Perfect_Party_Logo	1M_Press_Release_Firstname_Lastname

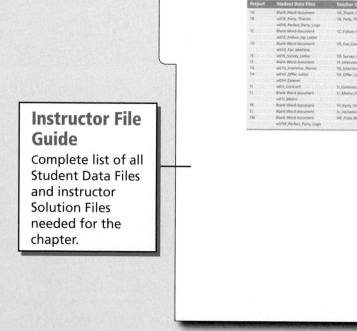

Instructor File Guide
Complete list of all Student Data Files and instructor Solution Files needed for the chapter.

Teach (continued)

Helpful Hints, Teaching Tips, Expand the Project

References correspond to what is being taught in the student textbook.

NEW

Full-Size Textbook Pages

An instructor copy of the textbook with traditional Instructor Manual content incorporated.

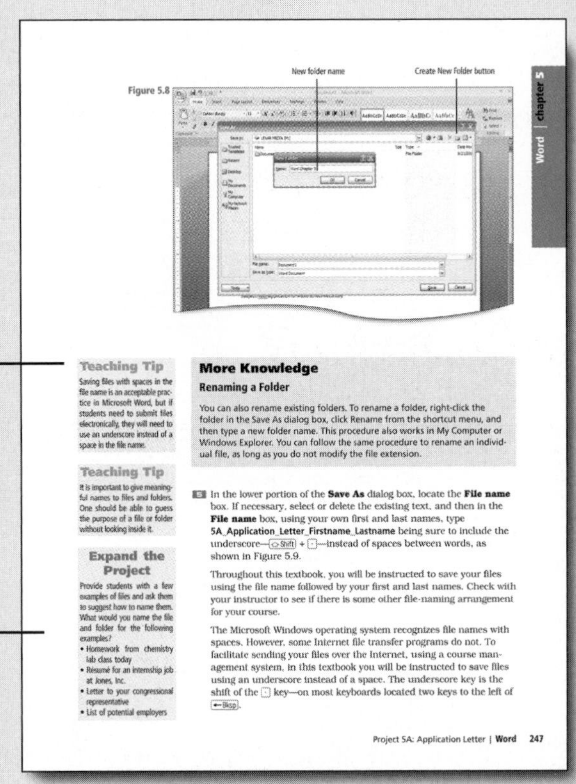

Figure 5.8

New folder name

Create New Folder button

Word | chapter 5

Teaching Tip

Saving files with spaces in the file name is an acceptable practice in Microsoft Word, but if students need to submit files electronically, they will need to use an underscore instead of a space in the file name.

Teaching Tip

It is important to give meaningful names to files and folders. One should be able to guess the purpose of a file or folder without looking inside it.

Expand the Project

Provide students with a few examples of files and ask them to suggest how to name them. What would you name the file and folder for the following examples?

- Homework from chemistry lab class today
- Résumé for an internship job at Jones, Inc.
- Letter to your congressional representative
- List of potential employers

More Knowledge

Renaming a Folder

You can also rename existing folders. To rename a folder, right-click the folder in the Save As dialog box, click Rename from the shortcut menu, and then type a new folder name. This procedure also works in My Computer or Windows Explorer. You can follow the same procedure to rename an individual file, as long as you do not modify the file extension.

5 In the lower portion of the **Save As** dialog box, locate the **File name** box. If necessary, select or delete the existing text, and then in the **File name** box, using your own first and last names, type **5A_Application_Letter_Firstname_Lastname** being sure to include the underscore—Shift + -—instead of spaces between words, as shown in Figure 5.9.

Throughout this textbook, you will be instructed to save your files using the file name followed by your first and last names. Check with your instructor to see if there is some other file-naming arrangement for your course.

The Microsoft Windows operating system recognizes file names with spaces. However, some Internet file transfer programs do not. To facilitate sending your files over the Internet, using a course management system, in this textbook you will be instructed to save files using an underscore instead of a space. The underscore key is the shift of the - key—on most keyboards located two keys to the left of Bksp.

Project 5A: Application Letter | Word 247

End-of-Chapter Concepts Assessments

contain the answers for quick reference.

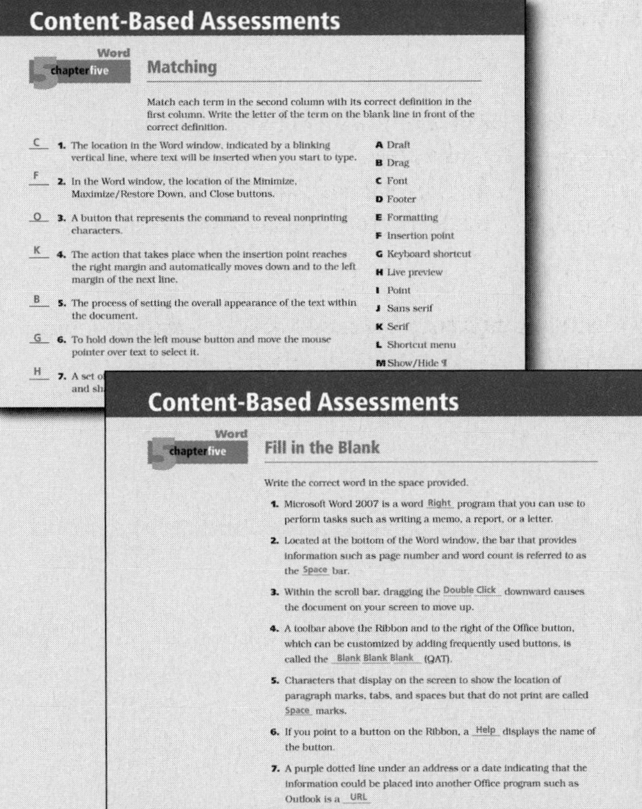

Content-Based Assessments

Word chapter five

Matching

Match each term in the second column with its correct definition in the first column. Write the letter of the term on the blank line in front of the correct definition.

C 1. The location in the Word window, indicated by a blinking vertical line, where text will be inserted when you start to type.

F 2. In the Word window, the location of the Minimize, Maximize/Restore Down, and Close buttons.

O 3. A button that represents the command to reveal nonprinting characters.

K 4. The action that takes place when the insertion point reaches the right margin and automatically moves down and to the left margin of the next line.

B 5. The process of setting the overall appearance of the text within the document.

G 6. To hold down the left mouse button and move the mouse pointer over text to select it.

H 7. A set of ... and sh...

A Draft
B Drag
C Font
D Footer
E Formatting
F Insertion point
G Keyboard shortcut
H Live preview
I Point
J Sans serif
K Serif
L Shortcut menu
M Show/Hide ¶

Content-Based Assessments

Word chapter five

Fill in the Blank

Write the correct word in the space provided.

1. Microsoft Word 2007 is a word Right program that you can use to perform tasks such as writing a memo, a report, or a letter.
2. Located at the bottom of the Word window, the bar that provides information such as page number and word count is referred to as the Space bar.
3. Within the scroll bar, dragging the Double Click downward causes the document on your screen to move up.
4. A toolbar above the Ribbon and to the right of the Office button, which can be customized by adding frequently used buttons, is called the Blank Blank Blank (QAT).
5. Characters that display on the screen to show the location of paragraph marks, tabs, and spaces but that do not print are called Space marks.
6. If you point to a button on the Ribbon, a Help displays the name of the button.
7. A purple dotted line under an address or a date indicating that the information could be placed into another Office program such as Outlook is a URL

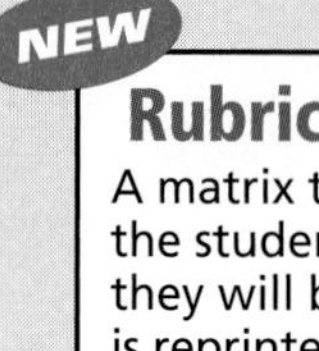

Rubric

A matrix to guide the student on how they will be assessed is reprinted in the Annotated Instructor Edition with suggested weights for each of the criteria and levels of performance. Instructors can modify the weights to suit their needs.

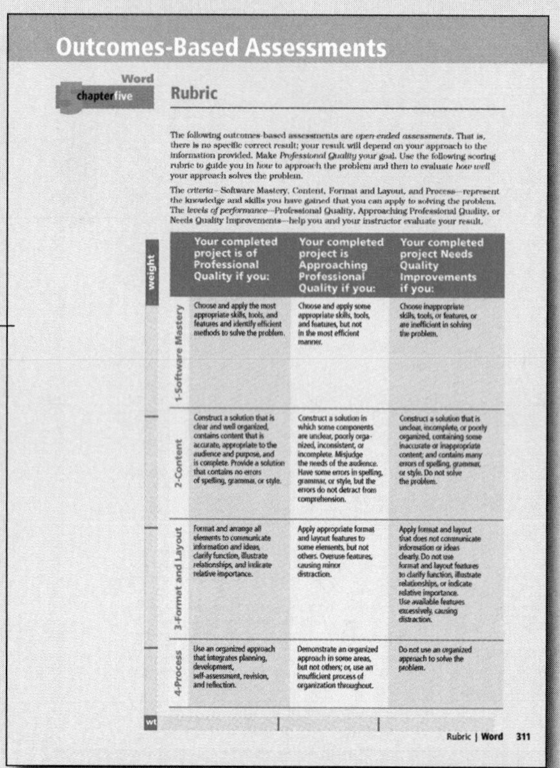

Outcomes-Based Assessments

Word chapterfive

Rubric

The following outcomes-based assessments are *open-ended assessments*. That is, there is no specific correct result; your result will depend on your approach to the information provided. Make *Professional Quality* your goal. Use the following scoring rubric to guide you in *how* to approach the problem and then to evaluate *how well* your approach solves the problem.

The *criteria*—Software Mastery, Content, Format and Layout, and Process—represent the knowledge and skills you have gained that you can apply to solving the problem. The *levels of performance*—Professional Quality, Approaching Professional Quality, or Needs Quality Improvements—help you and your instructor evaluate your result.

weight	Your completed project is of Professional Quality if you:	Your completed project is Approaching Professional Quality if you:	Your completed project Needs Quality Improvements if you:
1-Software Mastery	Choose and apply the most appropriate skills, tools, and features and identify efficient methods to solve the problem.	Choose and apply some appropriate skills, tools, and features, but not in the most efficient manner.	Choose inappropriate skills, tools, or features, or are inefficient in solving the problem.
2-Content	Construct a solution that is clear and well organized, contains content that is accurate, appropriate to the audience and purpose, and is complete. Provide a solution that contains no errors of spelling, grammar, or style.	Construct a solution in which some components are unclear, poorly organized, inconsistent, or incomplete. Misjudge the needs of the audience. Have some errors in spelling, grammar, or style, but the errors do not detract from comprehension.	Construct a solution that is unclear, incomplete, or poorly organized, containing some inaccurate or inappropriate content; and contains many errors of spelling, grammar, or style. Do not solve the problem.
3-Format and Layout	Format and arrange all elements to communicate information and ideas, clarify function, illustrate relationships, and indicate relative importance.	Apply appropriate format and layout features to some elements, but not others. Overuse features, causing minor distraction.	Apply format and layout that does not communicate information or ideas clearly. Do not use format and layout features to clarify function, illustrate relationships, or indicate relative importance. Use available features excessively, causing distraction.
4-Process	Use an organized approach that integrates planning, development, self-assessment, revision, and reflection.	Demonstrate an organized approach in some areas, but not others; or, use an insufficient process of organization throughout.	Do not use an organized approach to solve the problem.
wt			

Rubric | **Word** 311

Assess

Assignment Tags

Scoring checklist for assignments. NEW Now also available for Problem-Solving projects.

GO! with Microsoft® Office 2007

Assignment Tags for GO! with Office 2007
Word Chapter 5

Name:
Professor:
Project: 5A
Course:

Task	Points	Your Score
Center text vertically on page	2	
Delete the word "really"	1	
Delete the words "try to"	1	
Replace "last" with "first"	1	
Insert the word "potential"	1	
Replace "John W. Diamond" with "Lucy Burrows"	2	
Change entire document to the Cambria font	2	
Change the first line of text to Arial Black 20 pt. font	2	
Bold the first line of text	2	
Change the 2nd through 4th lines to Arial 10 pt.	2	
Italicize the 2nd through 4th lines of text	2	
Correct/Add footer as instructed	2	
Circled information is incorrect or formatted incorrectly		
Total Points	20	0

Name:
Professor:
Project: 5B
Course:

Task	Points	Your Score
Insert the file w05B_Music_School_Records	4	
Insert the Music Logo	4	
Remove duplicate "and"	2	
Change spelling and grammar errors (4)	8	
Correct/Add footer as instructed	2	
Circled information is incorrect or formatted incorrectly		
Total Points	20	0

Name:
Professor:
Project: 5C
Course:

Task	Points	Your Score
Add four line letterhead	2	
Insert today's date	1	
Add address block, subject line, and greeting	2	
Add two-paragraph body of letter	2	
Add closing, name, and title	2	
In subject line, capitalize "receipt"	1	
Change "standards" to "guidelines"	1	
Insert "quite"	1	
Insert "all"	1	
Change the first line of text to Arial Black 20 pt. font	2	
Bold the first line of text	1	
Change the 2nd through 4th lines to Arial 10 pt.	1	
Italicize the 2nd through 4th lines of text	1	
Correct/add footer as instructed	2	
Circled information is incorrect or formatted incorrectly		
Total Points	20	0

Name:
Professor:
Project: 5D
Course:

Task	Points	Your Score
Insert the file w05D_Marketing	4	
Bold the first two title lines	2	
Correct spelling of "Marketting"	2	
Correct spelling of "geners"	2	
Correct all misspellings of "allready"	2	
Correct grammar error "are" to "is"	2	
Insert the Piano image	4	
Correct/add footer as instructed	2	
Circled information is incorrect or formatted incorrectly		
Total Points	20	0

Highlighted Overlays

Solution files provided as transparency overlays. Yellow highlights point out the gradable elements for quick and easy grading.

Music School Records ← 20 point Arial Black, bold and underline

2620 Vine Street
Los Angeles, CA 90028 ← 10 point Arial, italic
323-555-0028

September 12, 2009

Text vertically centered on page

Body of document changed to Cambria font, 11 point

Mr. William Hawken
123 Eighth Street
Harrisville, MI 48740

Dear William:

Subject: Your Application to Music School Records

Thank you for submitting your application to Music School Records. Our talent scout for Northern Michigan, Catherine McDonald, is very enthusiastic about your music, and the demo CD you submitted certainly confirms her opinion.

Word "really" deleted

We discuss our applications from potential clients during the first week of each month. We will have a decision for you by the second week of October.

Words "try to" deleted

Yours Truly,

Lucy Burroughs

Point-Counted Production Tests (PCPTs)

A cumulative exam for each **project**, **chapter**, and **application**. Easy to score using the provided checklist with suggested points for each task.

GO! with Microsoft® Office 2007 Introductory

Point-Counted Production Test—Project for GO! with Microsoft® Office 2007 Introductory Project 5A

Instructor Name: ____________________

Course Information: ____________________

1. Start Word 2007 to begin a new blank document. Save your document as 5A_Cover_Letter_Firstname_Lastname Remember to save your file frequently as you work.
2. If necessary, display the formatting marks. With the insertion point blinking in the upper left corner of the document to the left of the default first paragraph mark, type the current date (you can use AutoComplete).
3. Press Enter three times and type the inside address:

   Music School Records

   2620 Vine Street

   Los Angeles, CA 90028
4. Press Enter three times, and type Dear Ms. Burroughs:

   Press Enter twice, and type Subject: Application to Music School Records

   Press Enter twice, and type the following text (skipping one line between paragraphs):

   I read about Music School Records in Con Brio magazine and I would like to inquire about the possibility of being represented by your company.

   I am very interested in a career in jazz and am planning to relocate to the Los Angeles area in the very near future. I would be interested in learning more about the company and about available opportunities.

   I was a member of my high school jazz band for three years. In addition, I have been playing in the local coffee shop for the last two years. My demo CD, which is enclosed, contains three of my most requested songs.

   I would appreciate the opportunity to speak with you. Thank you for your time and consideration. I look forward to speaking with you about this exciting opportunity.
5. Press Enter three times, and type the closing Sincerely, Press enter four times, and type your name.
6. Insert a footer that contains the file name.
7. Delete the first instance of the word *very* in the second body paragraph, and insert the word modern in front of *jazz*.

Copyright © 2008 Pearson Prentice Hall

Page 1 of 1

Test Bank

Available as TestGen Software or as a Word document for customization.

Chapter 5: Creating Documents with Microsoft Word 2007

Multiple Choice:

1. With word processing programs, how are documents stored?

A. On a network

B. On the computer

C. Electronically

D. On the floppy disk

Answer: C **Reference:** Objective 1: Create and Save a New Document **Difficulty:** Moderate

2. Because you will see the document as it will print, ________ view is the ideal view to use when learning Microsoft Word 2007.

A. Reading

B. Normal

C. Print Layout

D. Outline

Answer: C **Reference:** Objective 1: Create and Save a New Document **Difficulty:** Moderate

3. The blinking vertical line where text or graphics will be inserted is called the:

A. cursor.

B. insertion point.

C. blinking line.

D. I-beam.

Answer: B **Reference:** Objective 1: Create and Save a New Document **Difficulty:** Easy

Solution Files–Application and PDF format

Music School Records

Music School Records discovers, launches, and develops the careers of young artists in classical, jazz, and contemporary music. Our philosophy is to not only shape, distribute, and sell a music product, but to help artists create a career that can last a lifetime. Too often in the music industry, artists are forced to fit their music to a trend that is short-lived. Music School Records does not just follow trends, we take a long-term view of the music industry and help our artists develop a style and repertoire that is fluid and flexible and that will appeal to audiences for years and even decades.

The music industry is constantly changing, but over the last decade, the changes have been enormous. New forms of entertainment such as DVDs, video games, and the Internet mean there is more competition for the leisure dollar in the market. New technologies give consumers more options for buying and listening to music, and they are demanding high quality recordings. Young consumers are comfortable with technology and want the music they love when and where they want it, no matter where they are or what they are doing.

Music School Records embraces new technologies and the sophisticated market of young music lovers. We believe that providing high quality recordings of truly talented artists make for more discerning listeners who will cherish the gift of music for the rest of their lives. The expertise of Music School Records includes:

- Insight into our target market and the ability to reach the desired audience
- The ability to access all current sources of music income
- A management team with years of experience in music commerce
- Innovative business strategies and artist development plans
- Investment in technology infrastructure for high quality recordings and business services

pagexxxix_top.docx

Online Assessment and Training

my**it**lab is Prentice Hall's new performance-based solution that allows you to easily deliver outcomes-based courses on Microsoft Office 2007, with customized training and defensible assessment. Key features of my**it**lab include:

A *true* "system" approach: my**it**lab content is the same as in your textbook.
Project-based *and* skills-based: Students complete real-life assignments.
Advanced reporting *and* gradebook: These include student click stream data.
***No* installation required:** my**it**lab is completely Web-based. You just need an Internet connection, small plug-in, and Adobe Flash Player.

Ask your Prentice Hall sales representative for a demonstration or visit:

www.prenhall.com/myitlab

chapterone
Getting Started with Windows XP

OBJECTIVES

At the end of this chapter you will be able to:

1. Get Started with Windows XP
2. Resize, Move, and Scroll Windows
3. Maximize, Restore, Minimize, and Close Windows
4. Create a New Folder
5. Copy, Move, Rename, and Delete Files
6. Find Files and Folders
7. Compress Files

OUTCOMES

Mastering these objectives will enable you to:

PROJECT 1A

Start Windows XP and Work with Windows, Folders, and Files

Windows XP is the software that coordinates the activities of your computer's hardware. Windows XP controls how your screen is displayed, how you open and close programs, and the startup, shutdown, and navigation procedures for your computer. It is useful to become familiar with the basic features of the Microsoft Windows operating system, especially working with the Start button and taskbar; opening, closing, moving, and resizing windows; and saving and managing files.

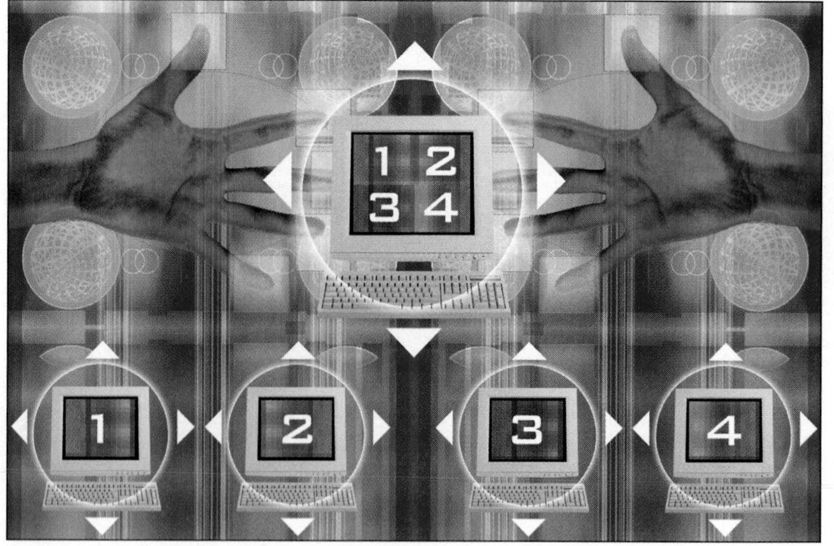

Getting Started with Windows XP

Project 1A Start Windows XP and Work with Windows, Folders, and Files

In Activities 1.1 through 1.9, you will practice navigating Windows XP. You will manage files and folders and compress and decompress files for easy file transfer. You will also capture an image of your screen, which will look similar to Figure 1.1.

For Project 1A, you will need the following files:

Flower.wmf
Plant.wmf
Roller Coaster.wmf
Golfer.wmf
Artist Picture.wmf
Lightning.docx
LSS-Charlotte NY Station.jpg
LSS-Crew Pulling Lifeboat.bmp
Volunteers.pptx
New blank Word document

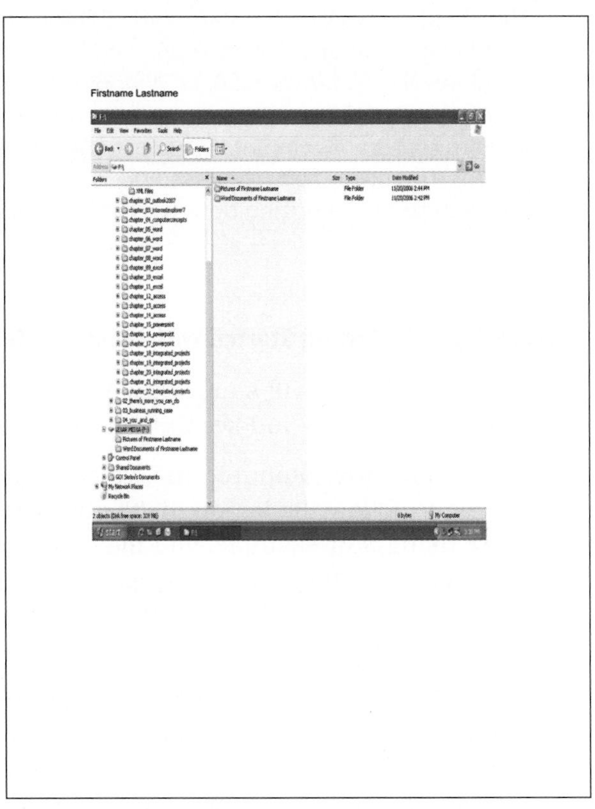

Figure 1.1
Project 1A—Windows XP

Objective 1
Get Started with Windows XP

Windows XP is an ***operating system***—software that controls the hardware attached to your computer including its memory, disk drive space, attached devices such as printers and scanners, and the central processing unit. Windows XP and earlier versions of Windows are similar; they use a ***graphical user interface (GUI)***. A GUI uses graphics or pictures to represent commands and actions and lets you see document formatting on the screen as it will look when printed on paper. ***Windows***, when spelled with a capital W, refers to the operating system that runs your computer.

Starting Windows is an automatic procedure; you turn on your computer, and after a few moments the version of Windows installed on your computer displays. Some versions require that you log in, and some do not. If you are using a different version of Windows, some procedures used in this chapter may work differently. Windows XP is available in two versions: a Professional Edition and a Home Edition. For basic tasks, the two versions work the same. The Professional version includes security and other features necessary in large organizations.

Alert!

Does your screen differ?

This chapter uses Windows XP Home Edition. When you see the word Windows, it will often be accompanied by the version, such as Windows 98, Windows NT, Windows 2000, or Windows XP, which is the version introduced in this chapter. These operating systems are similar and use graphics or pictures to represent commands and actions. Different versions may result in screens that differ from those shown in this chapter. Your screen may also differ because of the setting options that have been selected for your computer.

Activity 1.1 Getting Started with Windows XP

In Activity 1.1, you will start Windows, use the mouse, and use the Start button to open the Windows Calculator program.

1. Turn on your computer and wait for the **Windows** program to display, or follow the log-on instructions required for the computer you are using. For example, you may have to click a name on a Welcome screen, or enter a user ID or password. If this is your home computer and you are the only user, it is likely that you need do nothing except wait for a few moments.

   The Windows ***desktop***, which is the working area of the Windows XP screen, displays. The working area is called a desktop because on it you can place electronic versions of things you have on your regular desk. The screen look will vary, depending on which version of Windows you are using and what you have on your own desktop.

2. Compare your Windows desktop with Figure 1.2 and then take a moment to study the Windows elements identified in the table in Figure 1.3.

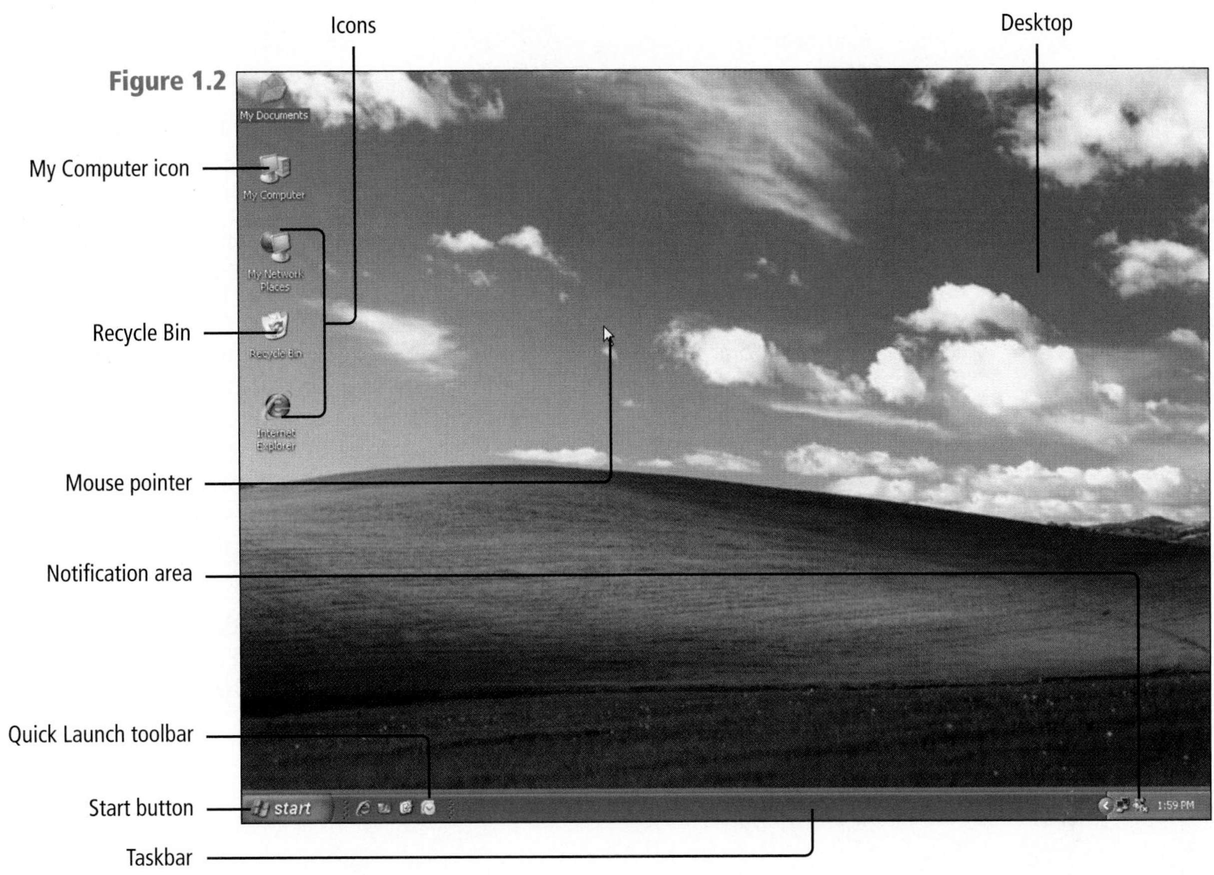

Windows Screen Elements	
Element	**Description**
Desktop	The working area of the Windows XP screen consisting of program icons, a taskbar, and a Start button.
Icon	A graphic representation of an object that you can select and open, such as a drive, a disk, a folder, a document, or a program.
Mouse pointer	The arrow, I-beam, or other symbol that moves when you move the mouse or other pointing device, and that indicates a location or position on your screen—also called the ***pointer***.
My Computer icon	An icon that represents the computer on which you are working, and that provides access to the drives, folders, and files on your computer.
Quick Launch toolbar	An area to the right of the Start button that contains shortcut icons for commonly used programs.

(*Continued*)

(Continued)

Element	Description
Recycle Bin	A temporary storage area for files that you have deleted. Files can be either recovered or permanently removed from the Recycle Bin.
Taskbar	Displays the Start button and the name of any open documents. The taskbar may also display shortcut buttons for other programs.
Notification area	The area on the right side of the taskbar, formerly called the ***system tray*** or ***status area***, where the clock and system notifications display. These notifications keep you informed about processes that are occurring in the background, such as antivirus software checking, network connections, and other utility programs. Some notifications display only temporarily.
Start button	The button on the left side of the taskbar that is used to start programs, change system settings, find Windows help, or shut down the computer.

Figure 1.3

3 Move the mouse across a flat surface to move the pointer on your screen. On the desktop, position the tip of the pointer in the center of the **My Computer** icon—referred to as ***pointing***. ***Double-click***—press the left mouse button two times in rapid succession—using caution not to move the mouse. If the My Computer icon is not visible, click the **Start** button start, and then from the displayed **Start** menu, click **My Computer**. Compare your screen with Figure 1.4 and then take a moment to study the My Computer window elements in Figure 1.5.

The My Computer window displays. A ***window***—spelled with a lowercase *w*—is a rectangular box that displays information or a program. When a window is open, the name of the window is displayed both in the title bar and in a button on the taskbar at the bottom of the desktop.

Figure 1.4

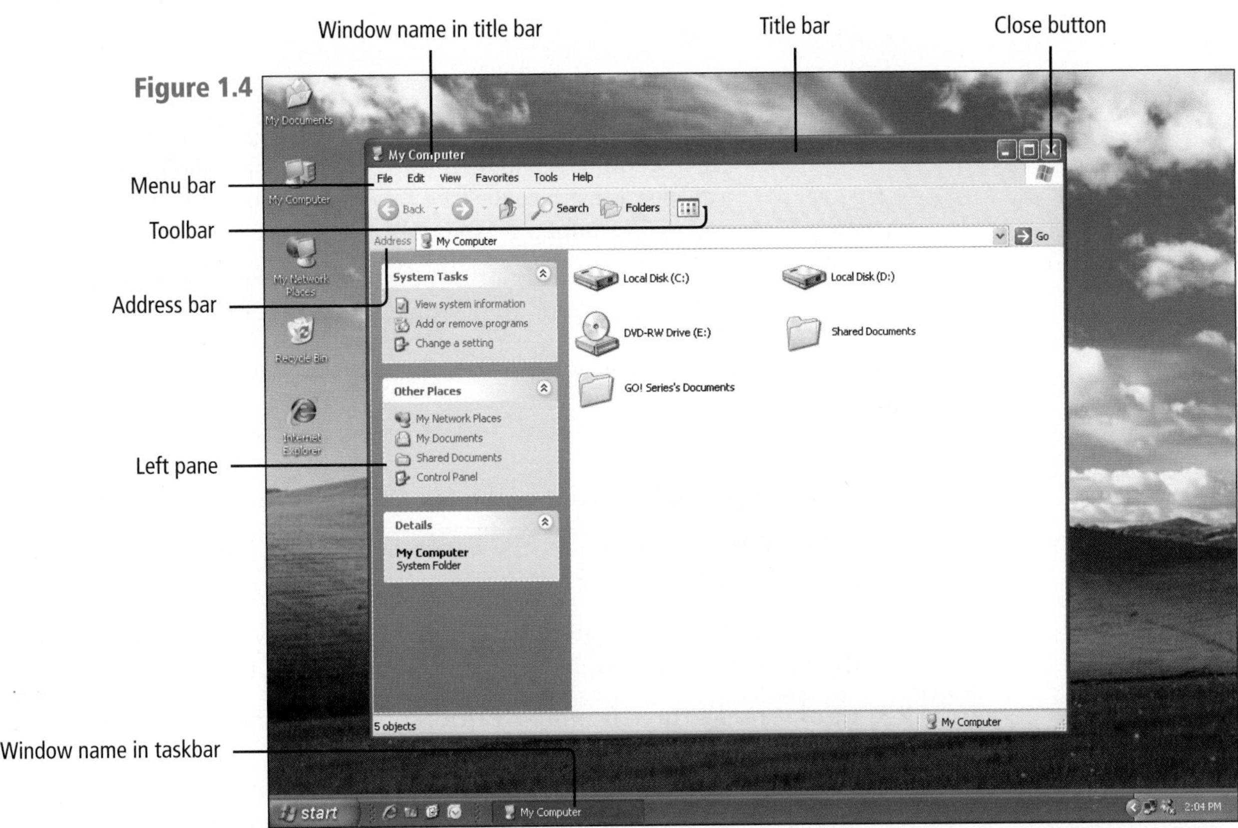

Parts of a Window

Screen Element	Description
Address bar	A toolbar that displays the organizational path to the active file, folder, or window.
Close button	A shortcut button in a title bar that closes a window or a program.
Left pane	In the My Computer window, a pane that displays information and commonly used tools.
Menu	A list of commands within a category.
Menu bar	The bar beneath the title bar that lists the names of menu categories, for example, *File*, *Edit*, *View*, and so on.
ScreenTip	A small box, activated by pointing to a button or other screen object, that displays the name of or further information about the screen element.
Status bar	A horizontal bar at the bottom of the document window that provides information about the current state of what you are viewing in the window, for example, the page number of a document.

(*Continued*)

Continued

Screen Element	Description
Title bar	Displays the program icon, the name of the document, and the name of the program. The Minimize, Maximize/Restore Down, and Close buttons are grouped on the right side of the title bar.
Toolbar	A row of buttons that activate commands, such as Undo or Bold, with a single click of the left mouse button.

Figure 1.5

4 In the upper right corner of the **My Computer** window title bar, point to, but do not click, the **Close** button and notice the ScreenTip *Close*.

A ***ScreenTip*** is a small note, usually in a yellow box, that provides the name of a button, or information about a screen element.

5 ***Click***—press the left mouse button one time—the **Close** button to close the **My Computer** window. Then, point to the **My Computer** icon on the desktop and click the right mouse button—this action is known as a ***right-click***. If the **My Computer** icon does not display on your desktop, click the **Start** button start, and then right-click **My Computer**. Compare your screen with Figure 1.6.

A shortcut menu displays. ***Shortcut menus*** list commands that are ***context-sensitive***—commands commonly used when working with the selected object. On this shortcut menu, the Open command is displayed in bold because it is the default action that occurs when you double-click this icon.

Figure 1.6

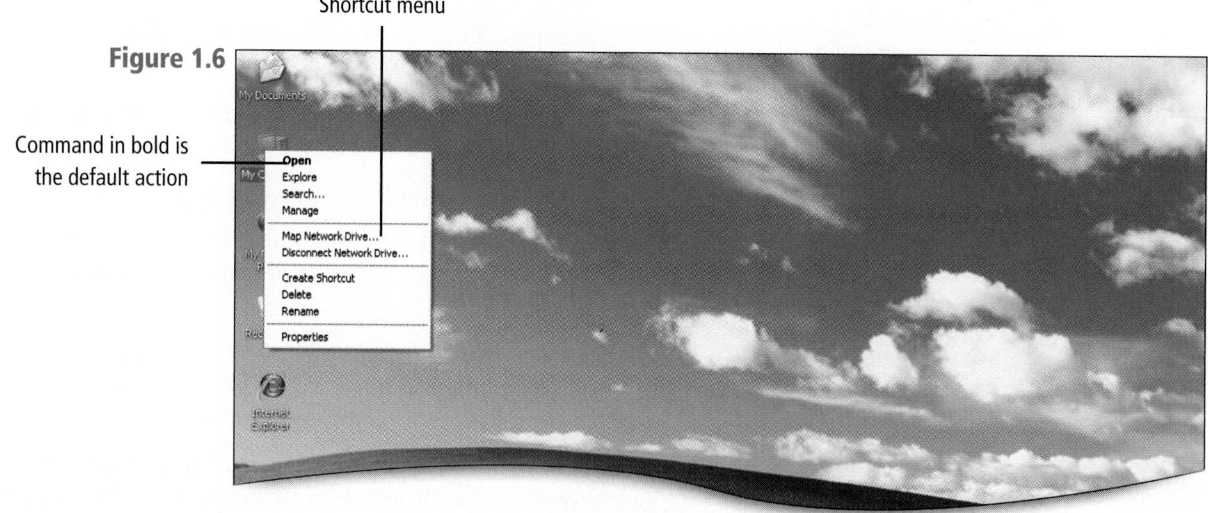

6 In the displayed shortcut menu, point to **Open** to highlight—select—the command, and then click. In the displayed **My Computer** window, point to and then click the disk drive labeled **Local Disk (C:)**, and then in the left pane, notice the lower panel. Compare your screen with Figure 1.7.

The specifications of the ***Local disk***—the large disk drive inside your computer system also referred to as the ***hard drive***—are displayed in the Details panel of the left pane. A ***drive*** is an area of storage that is formatted with the Windows file system and that has a drive letter such as C, D, E, and so on. If the Details panel does not display any information, click the expand/hide arrow next to Details to expand this panel of the task pane.

Figure 1.7

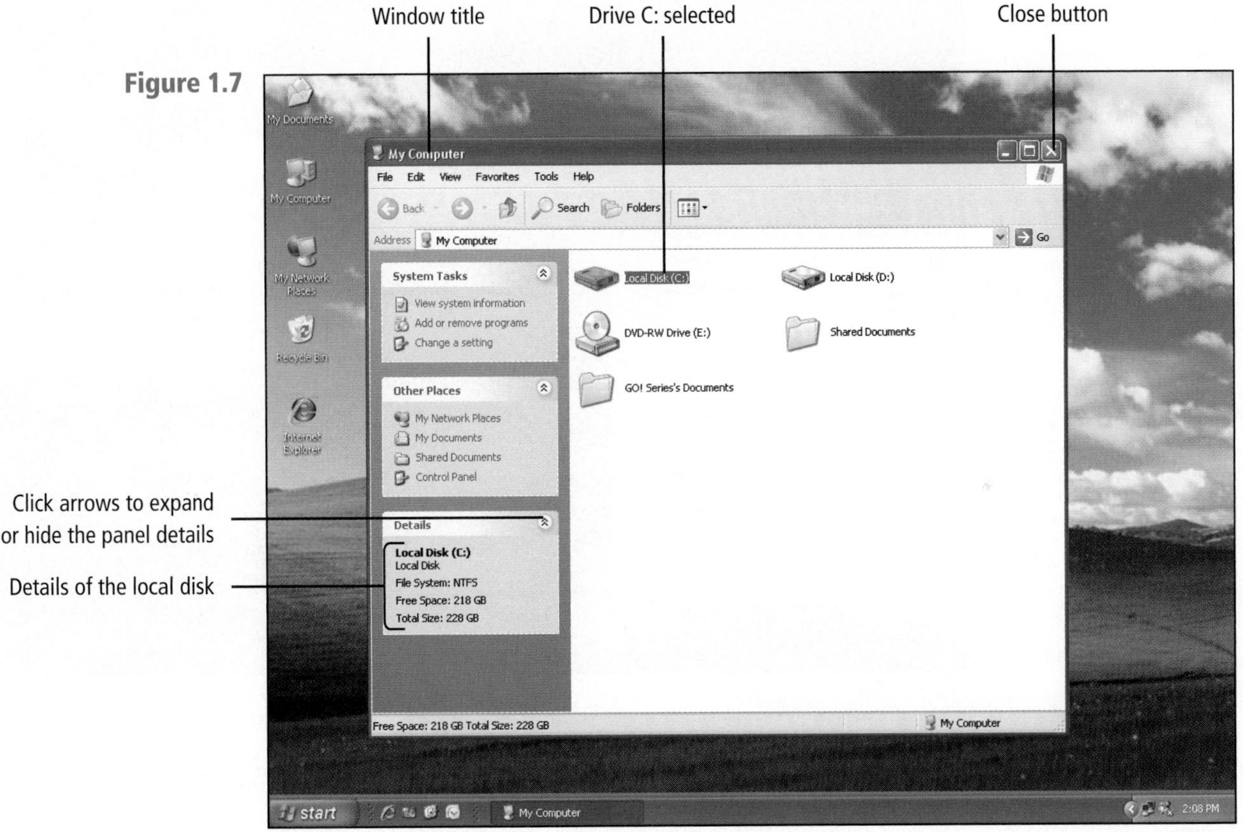

7 In the **My Computer** window title bar, click the **Close** button. In the lower left corner of the screen, point to, and then click the **Start** button. Compare your screen with Figure 1.8.

Commands in the displayed Start menu that have arrows on the right indicate that a submenu is available for a command. A ***submenu*** is a second-level menu. You can customize the Start menu to include shortcuts to programs and files you use often.

Figure 1.8

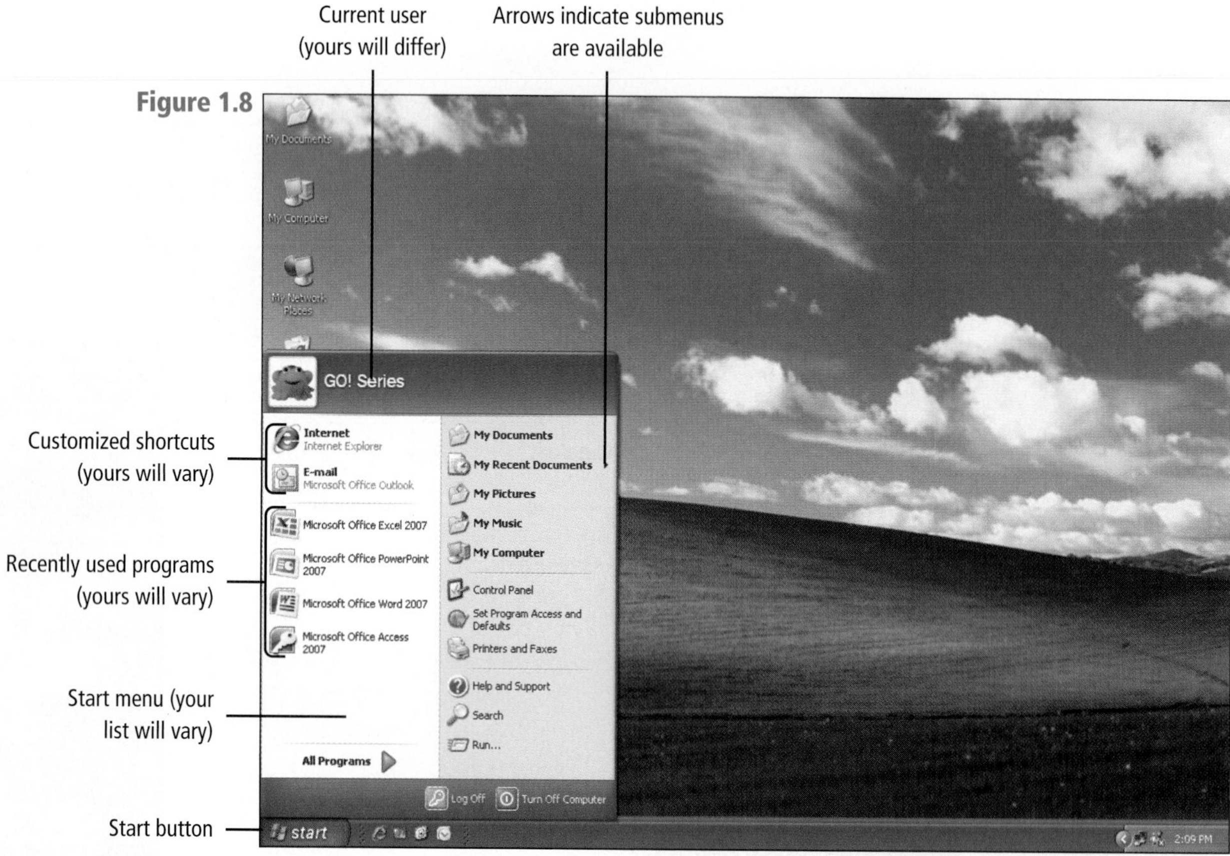

8 On the **Start** menu, point to, but do not click, the **All Programs** command.

The All Programs submenu displays. Your menu will differ from the one shown in Figure 1.9 because your computer will have different programs installed. Folders in the menu contain more programs, or more folders, or some of each. A small arrow to the right of a folder indicates that the folder contains other folders or zipped—compressed—files.

9 On the **All Programs** menu, point to, but do not click, **Accessories**.

Figure 1.9

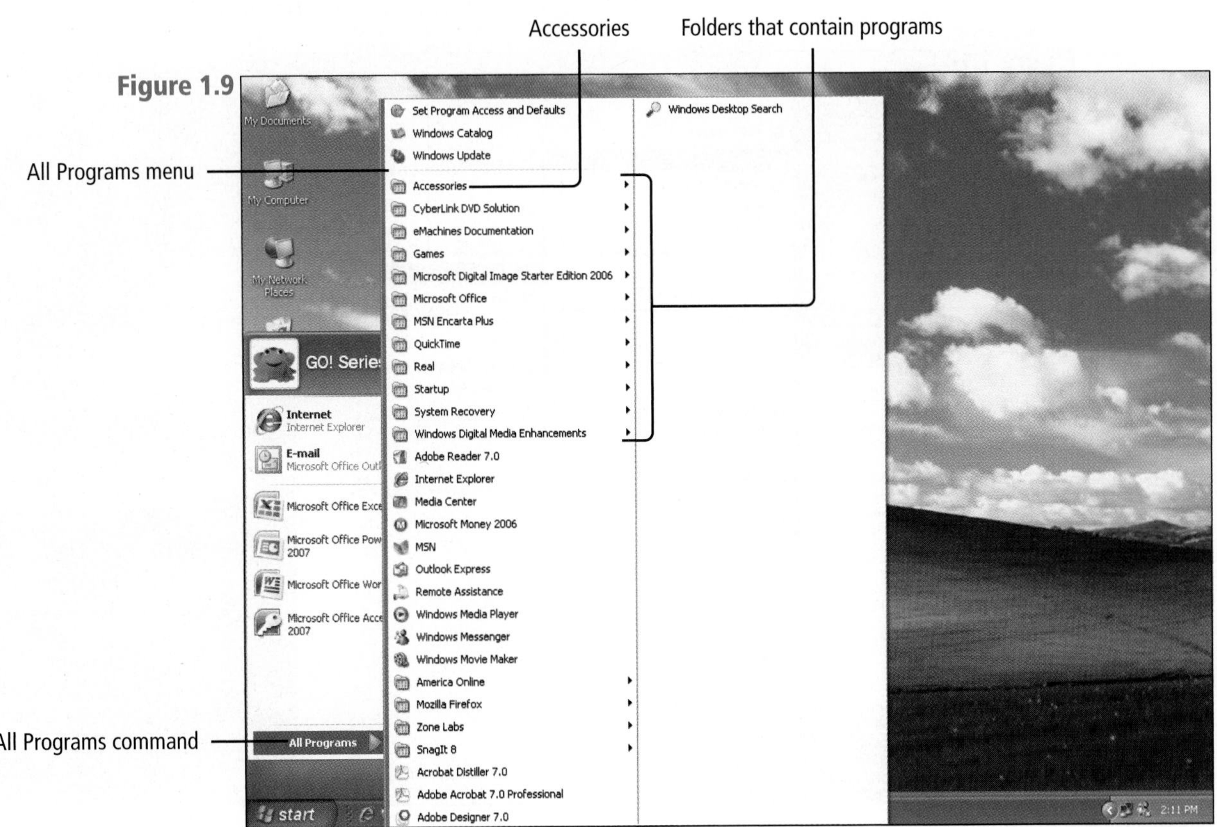

10 In the displayed **Accessories** submenu, point to **Calculator** as shown in Figure 1.10, and notice the displayed ScreenTip, *Performs basic arithmetic tasks with an on-screen calculator.*

You can access the Accessories programs from the Start menu and use them while you are using other Office programs. For example, you may want to make a quick calculation while you are typing a document in Microsoft Word. You can open the calculator, make the calculation, and then place the result in your Word document without closing Word.

Figure 1.10

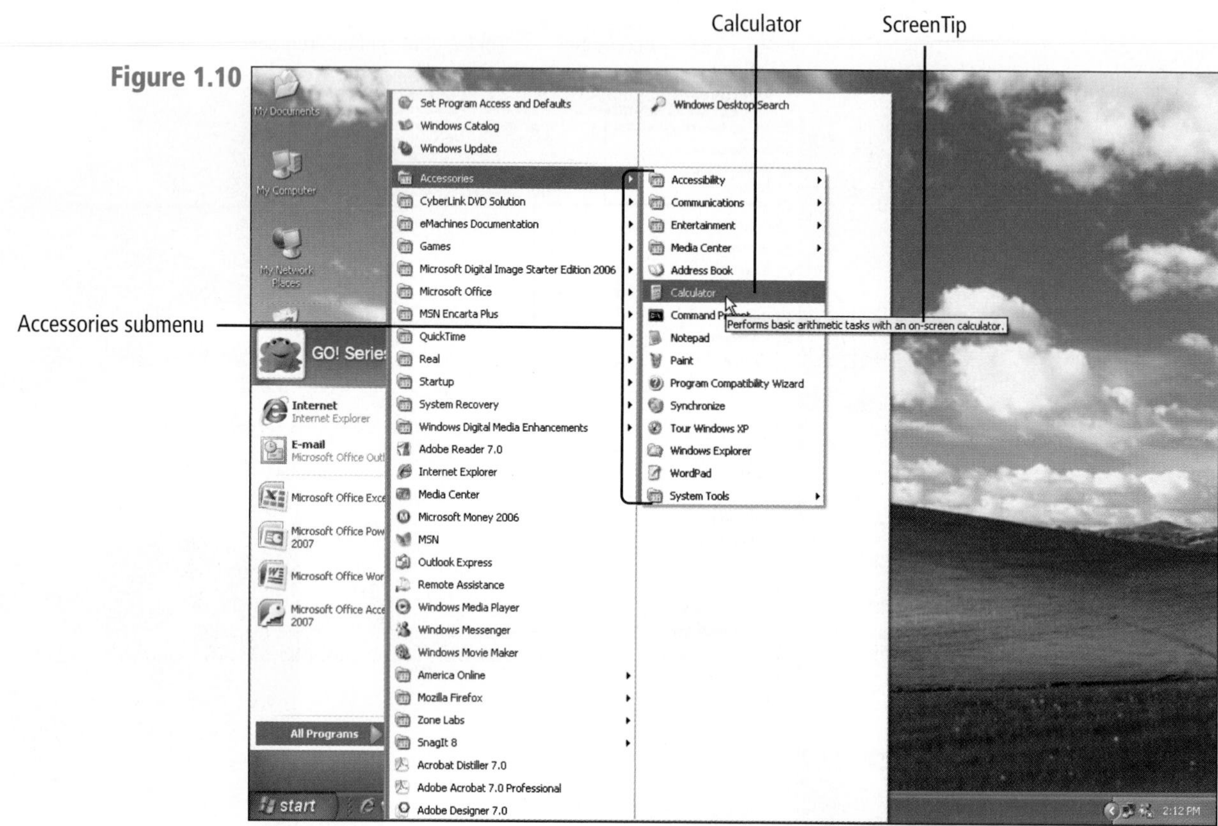

11 Click the **Calculator** command to open the Calculator window and close the **Start** menu. Then, practice using the calculator, which is shown in Figure 1.11. Point to click numbers and keys exactly as you would press keys on a calculator.

Figure 1.11

12 On the **Calculator** title bar, click the **Close** button.

Objective 2
Resize, Move, and Scroll Windows

When a window opens on your screen, it generally opens in the same size and shape as it was when last used. If you are using more than one window at a time, you can increase or decrease the size of a window, or move a window so that you can see the information you need.

As you work within a program, the information you create will often grow larger than the screen can display. When the information in a window extends beyond the lower or right edges of the window, scroll bars display at the lower and right side of the window. Using the ***horizontal scroll bar***, you can move left and right to view information that extends beyond the left or right edge of the screen. Using the ***vertical scroll bar***, you can move up and down to view information that extends beyond the top or bottom of the screen.

Activity 1.2 Resizing, Moving, and Scrolling Windows

In Activity 1.2, you will open, resize, and move the My Computer window. You will also use the scroll bars in the My Computer window to view information that does not fit on the screen.

1. On the **Windows** desktop, double-click the **My Computer** icon to open the **My Computer** window. Alternatively, right-click the icon and click Open.

2. Check to see if the **My Computer** window opened as shown in 1.12, or if it opened and fills the entire screen. If the My Computer window fills the entire screen, on the right side of the title bar, click the **Restore Down** button .

3. Move the pointer to the lower right corner of the window to display the diagonal resize pointer , and then compare your screen with Figure 1.12.

   When the mouse pointer is in this shape, you can use it to change the size and shape of a window.

Figure 1.12

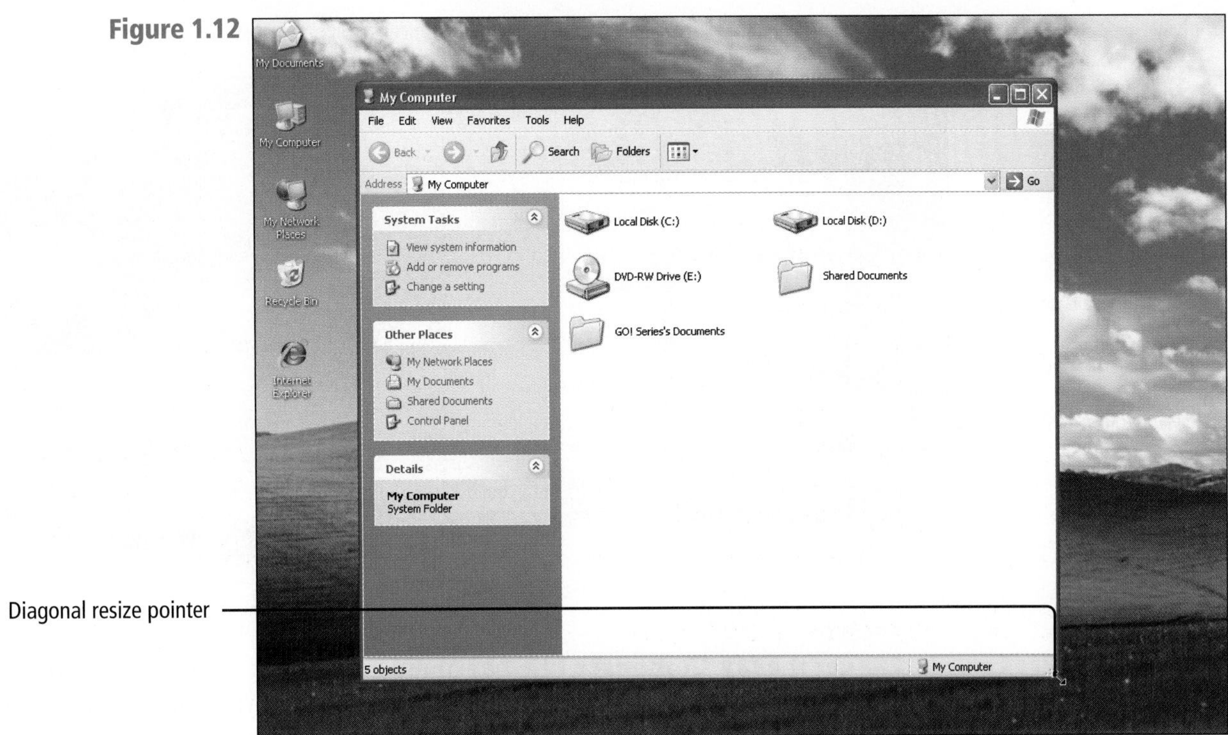

4 Hold down the left mouse button, ***drag***—move the mouse while holding down the left mouse button, and then release at the appropriate time—diagonally up and to the left until you see a scroll bar at both the bottom and right sides. Adjust as necessary so that the My Computer window is the approximate size of the one shown in Figure 1.13. Adjust as necessary to be sure that scroll bars display.

Scroll bars display on the right side and at the bottom of the window. A scroll bar is added to the window whenever the window contains more than it can display.

Figure 1.13

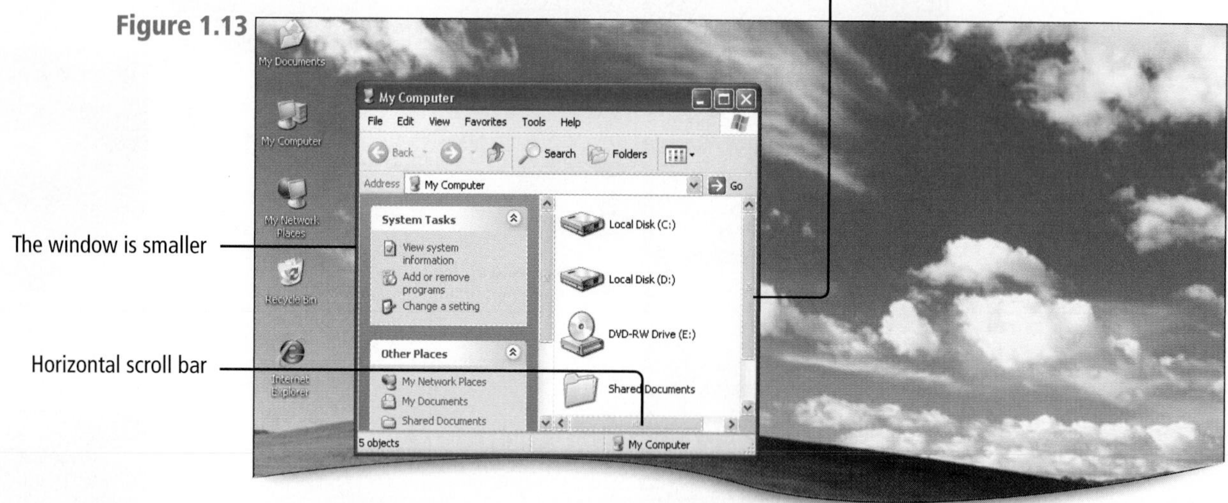

5 On the **My Computer** title bar, point to a blank area. Hold down the left mouse button, drag—hold down the left mouse button, move the mouse, and then release the mouse button—down approximately 2 inches and to the right approximately 2 inches. Compare your screen with Figure 1.14.

When you release the mouse button, the window drops into the new location. Use this technique to move an open window on your screen.

Figure 1.14

6 At the bottom of the vertical scroll bar, point to the **down arrow** and click, and notice that information at the bottom of the window scrolls up so that you can see the folders and icons that were not visible before, as shown in Figure 1.15.

Figure 1.15

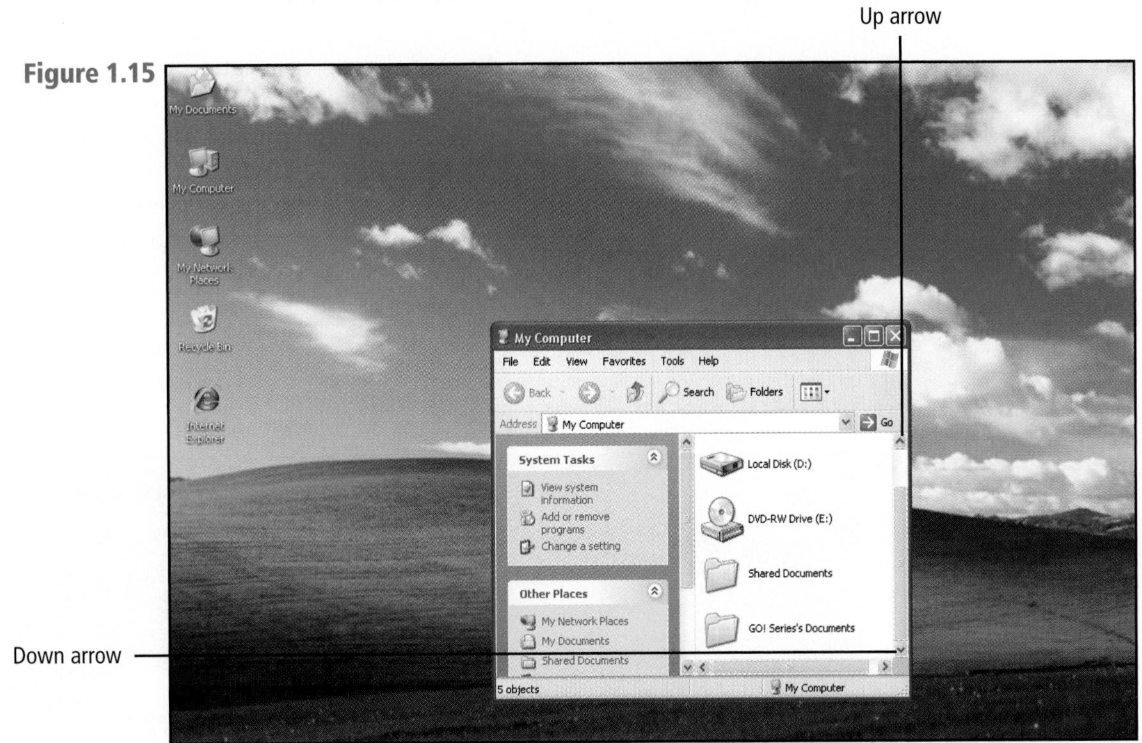

7 Point to the **up arrow** on the same scroll bar, and then click and hold down the left mouse button.

The list scrolls up until the first item is displayed. You can click and hold down the left mouse button on the up or down scroll arrow to scroll rapidly through a long list of information.

8 Point to the scroll box, as shown in Figure 1.16, and then drag it downward.

The ***scroll box*** displays within the vertical and horizontal scroll bars and provides a visual indication of your location within the information displayed. It can also be used with the mouse to reposition the information on the screen. The size of the scroll box varies to indicate the relative size of the information. Moving the scroll box gives you more control as you scroll because you can see the information as it moves up or down in the window.

You can move up or down a screen at a time by clicking in the area above or below the vertical scroll box. You can also move left or right a screen at a time by clicking in the area to the left or right of the horizontal scroll box. The size of the scroll box indicates the relative size of the display to the whole document. If the scroll box is small, it means that the display is a small portion of the whole document.

Figure 1.16

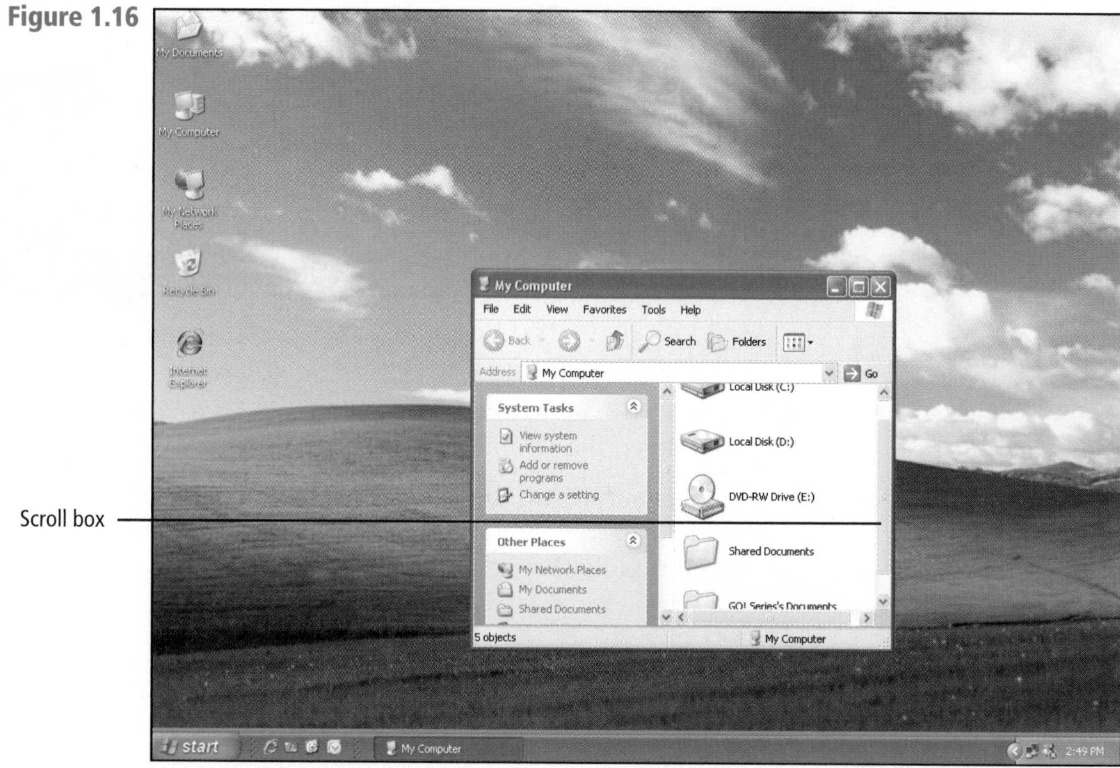

9 Move the pointer to the upper edge of the **My Computer** window to display the vertical resize pointer . Drag the top edge of the window to approximately 1 inch below the top of the screen.

10 Move the pointer to the left edge of the **My Computer** window to display the horizontal resize pointer . Drag the left side of the window to within approximately 1 inch of the left side of the screen.

You can see that by resizing the corners and sides of a window, and by dragging the window to different positions on the screen by the title bar, you have plenty of freedom to move and size any window to make it easier to use.

Objective 3
Maximize, Restore, Minimize, and Close Windows

You can ***maximize*** a window, which enlarges the window to occupy the entire screen, and you can ***restore*** a window, which reduces the window to the size it was before being maximized. You can also ***minimize*** a window, which reduces the window to a button on the taskbar, removing it from the screen entirely without actually closing it. When you need to view the window again, you can click the taskbar button to bring it back into view.

Activity 1.3 Maximizing, Restoring, Minimizing, and Closing a Window

In Activity 1.3, you will maximize, restore, minimize, and close the My Computer window.

1 In the upper right corner of the **My Computer** window, on the **My Computer** title bar, point to the **Maximize** button , and then compare your screen with Figure 1.17.

The Maximize button is the middle button in the group of three. When you point to it, a ScreenTip displays. Recall that a ScreenTip describes a button or screen element.

Figure 1.17

2 Click the **Maximize** button, and then compare your screen with Figure 1.18. Alternatively, maximize or restore a window by double-clicking anywhere in the window's title bar.

The My Computer window occupies the entire screen. The Maximize button is replaced by the Restore Down button, which has a different icon.

Figure 1.18

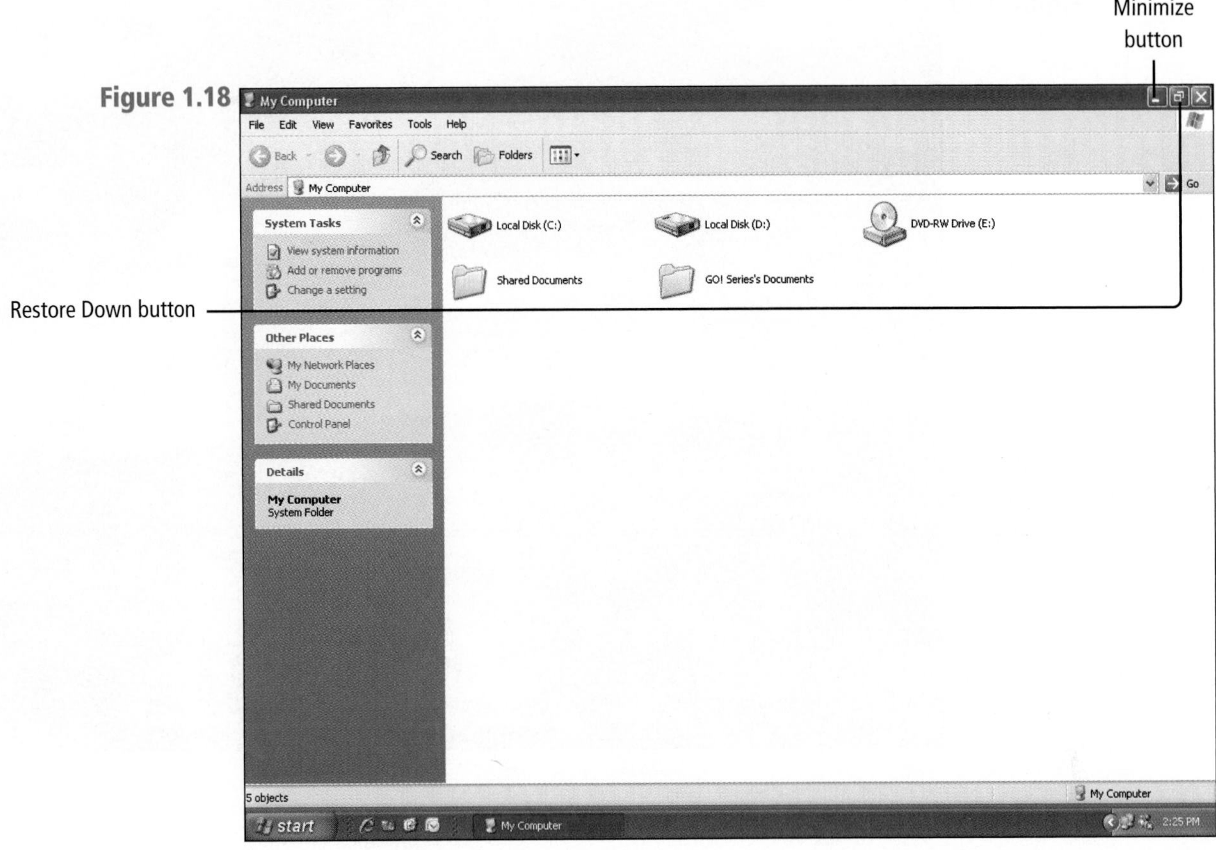

3 On the **My Computer** title bar, click the **Restore Down** button to return the window to the size it was before it was maximized.

4 On the **My Computer** title bar, click the **Minimize** button, and then compare your screen with Figure 1.19.

The My Computer program is still running but the window is minimized. It is represented by a button on the taskbar at the bottom of the screen. The window is not closed, only temporarily hidden from view.

Figure 1.19

My Computer window minimized to a button on the taskbar

5 On the taskbar, click the **My Computer** button.

The window redisplays in the same size and location it occupied when you clicked the Minimize button.

6 On the taskbar, click the **Start** button start, point to **All Programs**, point to **Accessories**, and then click **Calculator**. Point to the **Calculator** window title bar and drag the Calculator window near the left side of the screen. Notice that both open programs display on the taskbar.

My Computer is a program that helps you manage and organize the space on drives attached to your computer. Calculator is a program that performs basic arithmetic. Both programs occupy their own window, with the Calculator program in front of the My Computer window. Calculator becomes the ***active window***. When two or more windows are open, the active window is the window in which the insertion point movements, commands, or text entry occur.

7 Click anywhere on the **My Computer** window, and notice that the **My Computer** window moves to the front, as shown in Figure 1.20.

Figure 1.20

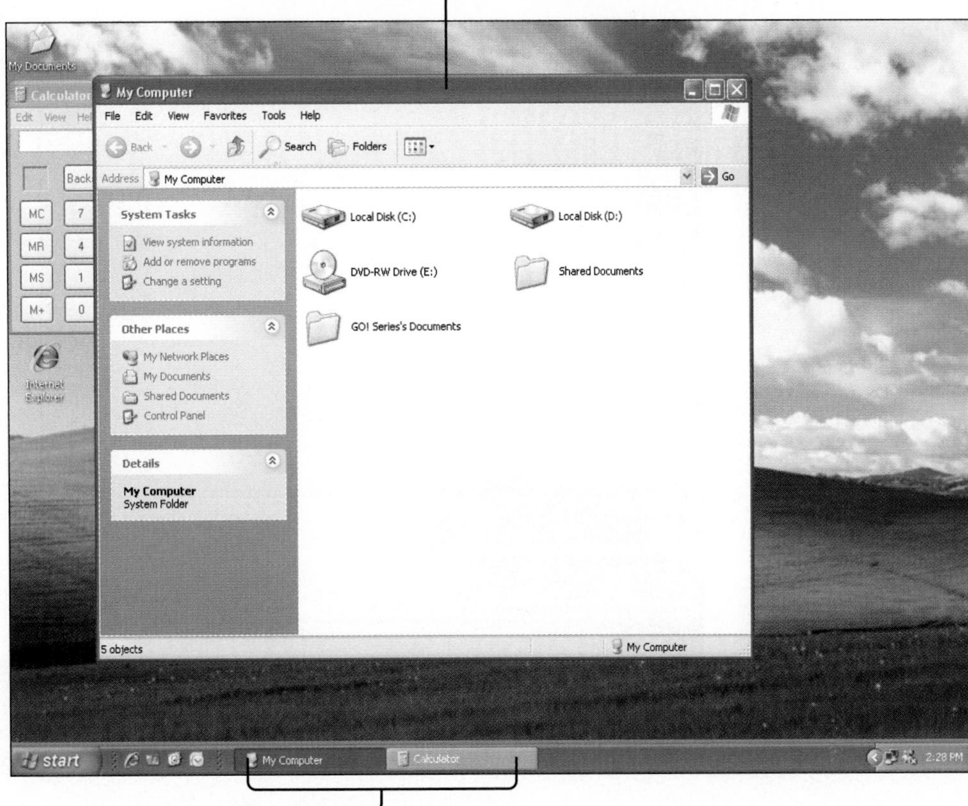

8 On the taskbar, click the **Calculator** button to move the calculator window to the front. On the taskbar, click the **Start** button [start], point to **All Programs**, point to **Accessories**, and then click **Paint**. Notice that all three open programs display on the taskbar, as shown in Figure 1.21.

Paint, a program that comes with Windows XP, creates and edits drawings and displays and edits scanned photos. The Calculator program window is still open, but it is likely hidden behind the other windows.

Figure 1.21

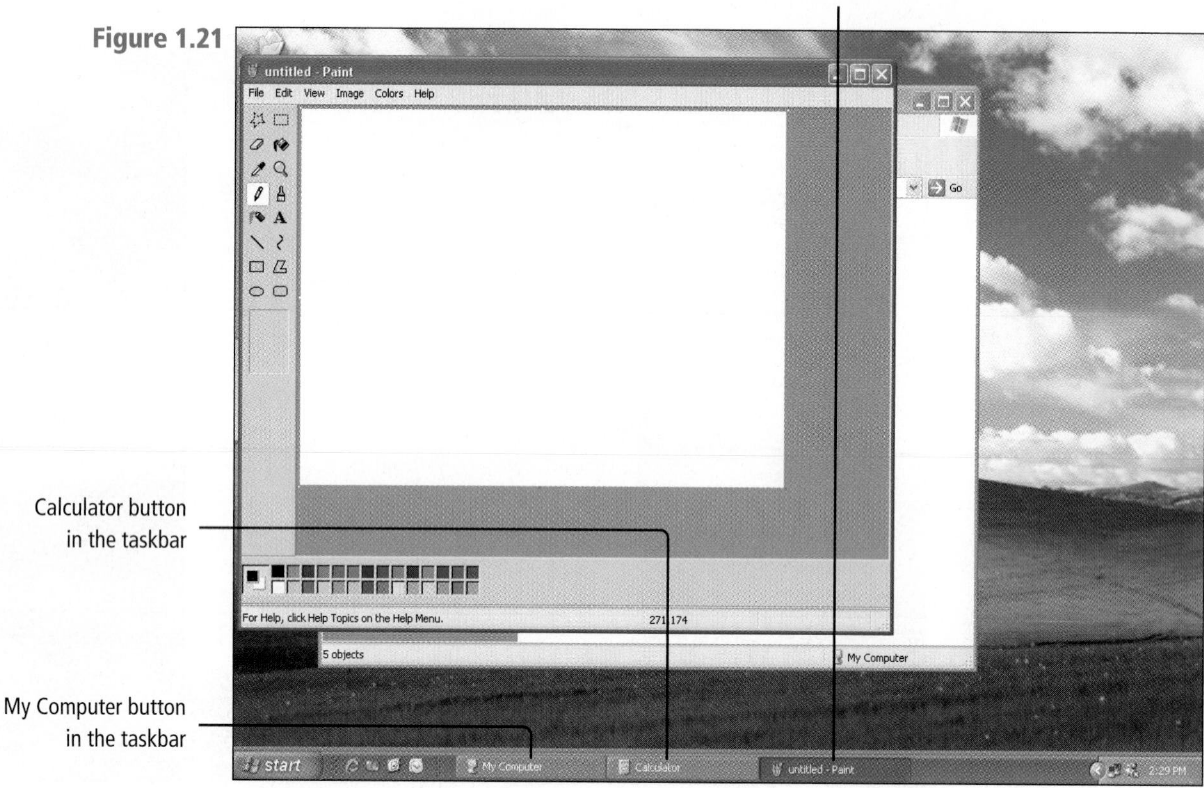

9 On the **Paint** title bar, click the **Close** button ☒. On the **Calculator** title bar, click the **Close** button ☒. On the **My Computer** window title bar, click the **Close** button ☒.

More Knowledge

Keeping More Than One Program Window Open at a Time

The ability to keep more than one window open at a time will become more useful as you become more familiar with Microsoft Office. For example, if you want to take information from two word processing documents to create a third document, you can open all three documents and use the taskbar to move among them, copying and pasting text from one document to another. Or, you could copy a chart from Excel and paste it into Word or take a table of data and paste it into PowerPoint. You can even have the same document open in two windows.

Objective 4
Create a New Folder

Information you create in a computer program is stored in the computer's memory, which is a temporary storage location. This data will be lost if the computer is turned off. To keep the information you create, you must save it as a file on one of the drives available to you. For example, a five-page term paper that you create in a word processing program such as Microsoft Word, when saved, is a ***file***. Files can be stored directly on a drive, but more commonly are stored in a folder on the drive. A ***folder*** is a container for programs and files and is represented on the screen by a picture of a common paper file folder.

Use folders to organize the location of your programs and files so that you can easily locate them for later use. Folders and files must be created and stored on one of the drives attached to your computer. Your available drives fall into three categories: 1) the nonremovable hard drive, also called the local disk, inside the computer; 2) removable drives that you insert into the computer such as a 3 $\frac{1}{2}$ inch floppy disk, a ZIP disk, a flash drive, or a writable CD; or 3) a shared network drive connected to your computer through a computer network, such as the network at your college.

Activity 1.4 Creating a New Folder

In Activity 1.4, you will create a folder on one of the three types of drives available to you—the local disk (hard drive), a removable drive (USB flash drive, ZIP disk, 3 $\frac{1}{2}$ inch floppy disk, or some other type of removable drive), or a network drive. If you are using a computer in a college lab, you may have space assigned to you on a shared network drive. You can create these folders on any drive that is available to you. The following activity assumes that you are saving your file to a USB flash drive.

1. Insert your USB flash drive or other removable drive. If an action dialog box displays asking what you want Windows to do, click **Cancel**. On the taskbar, click the **Start** button start, and then click **My Computer** to open the **My Computer** window. In the **My Computer** title bar, click the **Maximize** button if the window is not already maximized.

   A ***dialog box*** is a window that displays and that asks you to make a decision about an individual object or topic.

2 On the Standard Buttons toolbar, click the **Folders** button, and then compare your screen to Figure 1.22. If you do not see a list of drives, in the left pane, click **My Computer**.

The left pane changes to the Folders task pane. A ***task pane*** is an area within an Office program that provides commonly used commands. Its location and small size enable you to use these commands while still working on your files. The Folders task pane displays the drives and folders on your computer. This task pane is useful when navigating among the drives and folders on your computer. A flash drive, labeled F: (your drive letter may be different) is visible in both the Folders task pane on the left and in the pane on the right. You can display the contents of a flash drive, which is used in this instruction, using either icon.

Figure 1.22

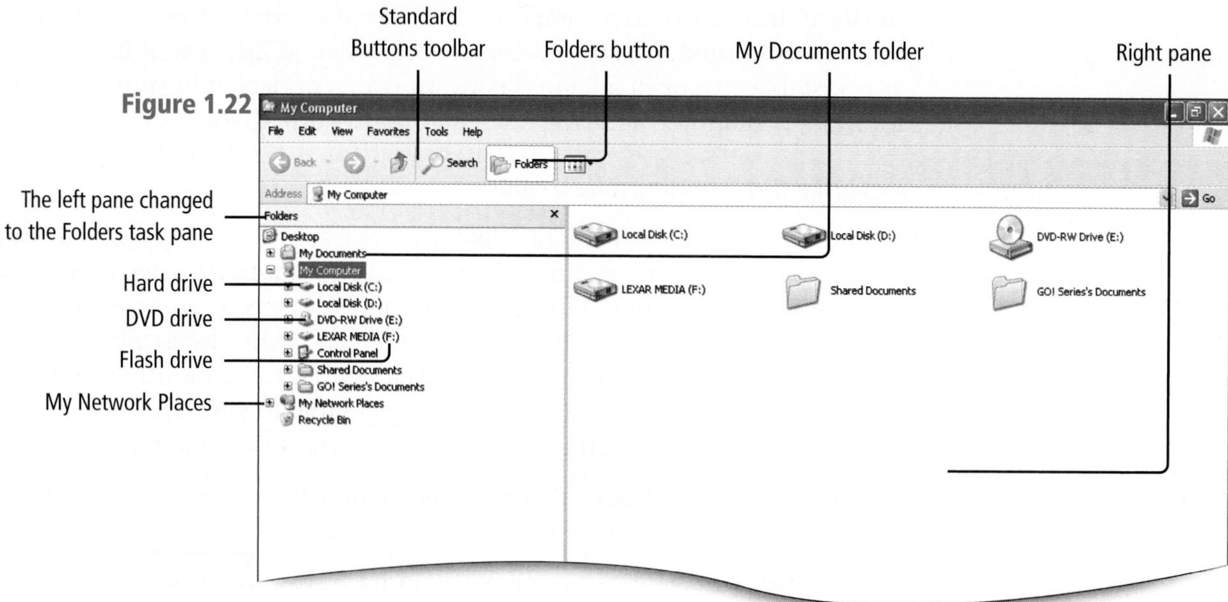

3 On the Standard Buttons toolbar, click the **Views** button, and then, if necessary, click **Tiles** to select this view option. Notice that icons and a brief description display in the right pane.

4 On the Standard Buttons toolbar, click the **Views** button, and then click **Details**.

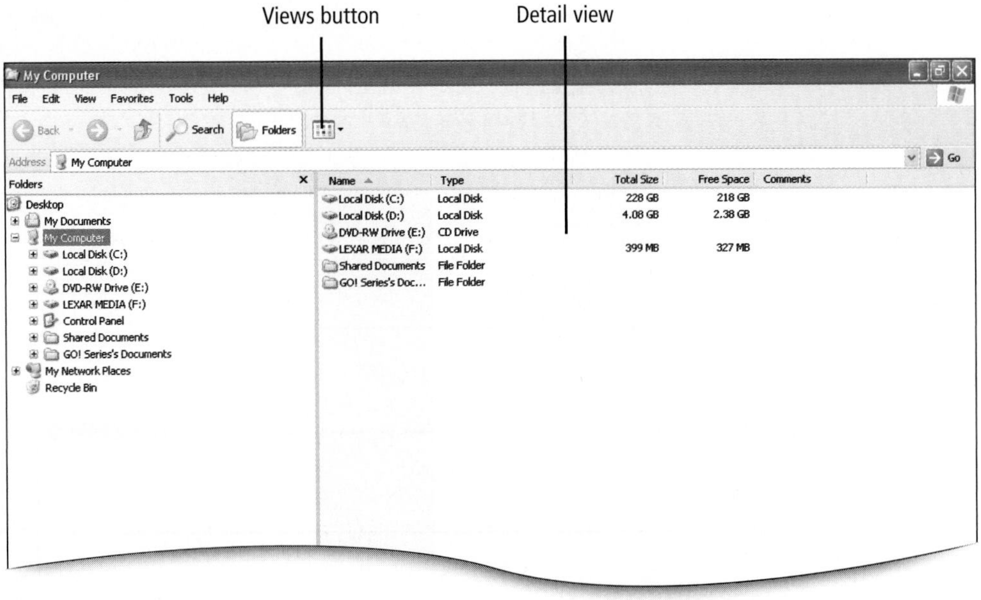

Views button

Detail view

Figure 1.23

The drives and folders display in a list format, with more information about the hard drive(s), as shown in Figure 1.23. The columns displayed on your computer may be different and may also be numbered differently.

5 In the **Folders** task pane, click the **USB flash drive** (or other removable media that you have inserted). For purposes of this instruction, the examples will indicate a USB flash drive, called LEXAR MEDIA (F:).

The contents of the drive are displayed in the right pane—in Figure 1.23, the drive is empty; your drive may contain files and folders. Your drive letter may also differ.

6 In the right pane, right-click in a blank area. In the displayed shortcut menu, point to the **New** command, and then compare your screen with Figure 1.24. Alternatively, from the **File** menu, click **New**.

A submenu displays, showing the various items that can be created using the New command.

Figure 1.24

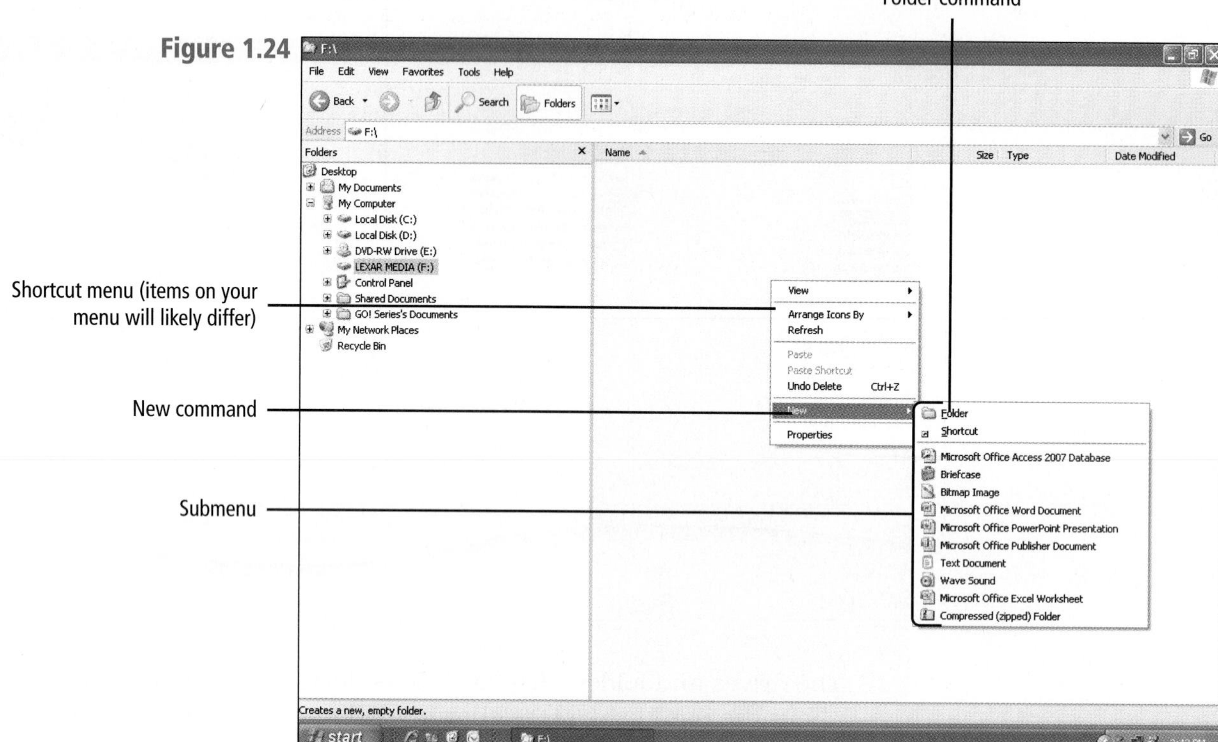

7 Click the **Folder** command, and then compare your screen with Figure 1.25.

A new folder—named *New Folder*—is created with the name of the folder displayed in the ***edit mode***. Edit mode enables you to change the name of a file or folder, and works the same in all Windows programs.

Figure 1.25

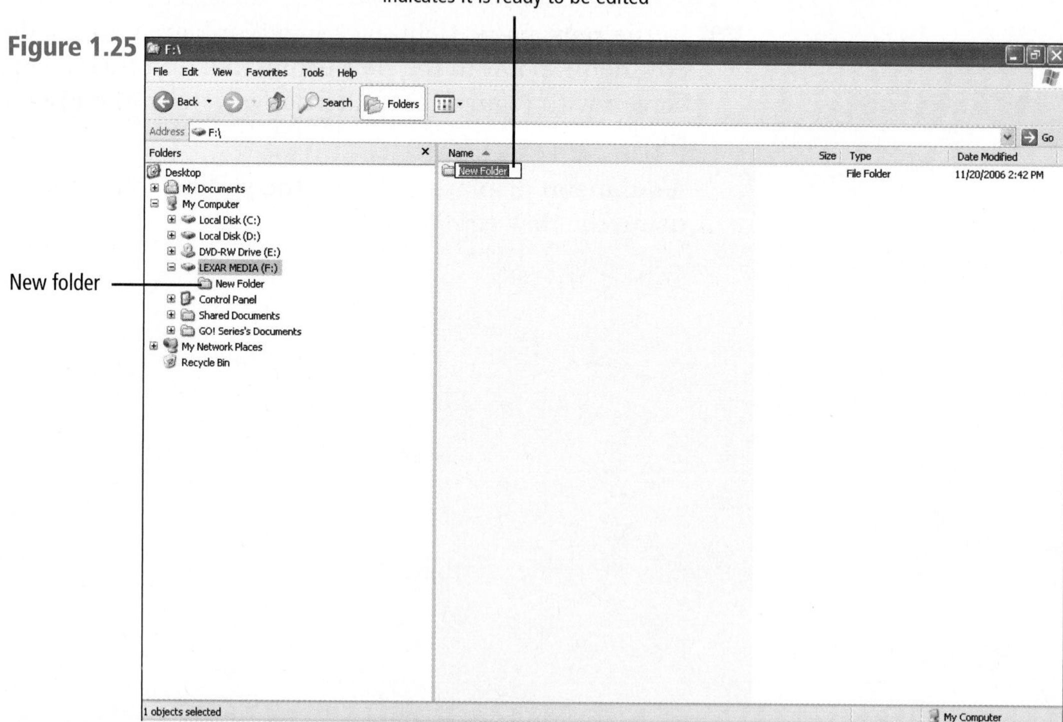

8 With **New Folder** selected in blue, substituting your name where indicated, type **Word Documents of Firstname Lastname** and press Enter. Then, click anywhere in the blank area of the right pane to deselect the new folder and then compare your screen with Figure 1.26.

Figure 1.26

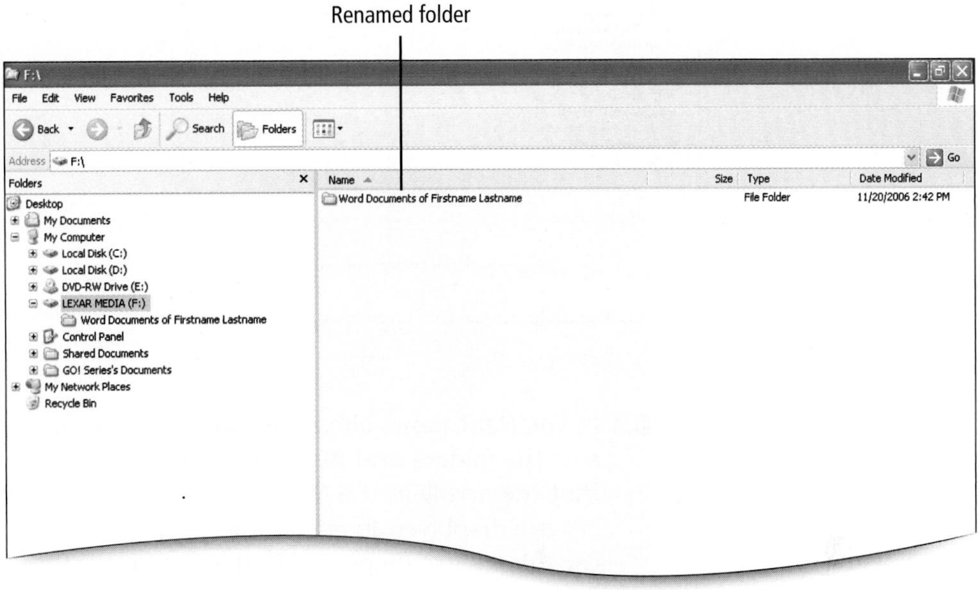

Renamed folder

Name	Size	Type	Date Modified
Word Documents of Firstname Lastname		File Folder	11/20/2006 2:42 PM

Another Way

To Rename a Folder

If you accidentally press Enter before you have a chance to name the folder, you can still rename it. Right-click the folder, click Rename from the shortcut menu, type a new name, and then press Enter. Alternatively, you can click the folder once, pause, and then click the folder again.

9 From the **File** menu, point to **New**, and then click **Folder**. Substituting your name where indicated, type **Pictures of Firstname Lastname** and press Enter. Compare your screen to Figure 1.27.

Two new folders have been created in your storage location. The folders are currently in the Details view. Notice the order in which the folders display.

Figure 1.27

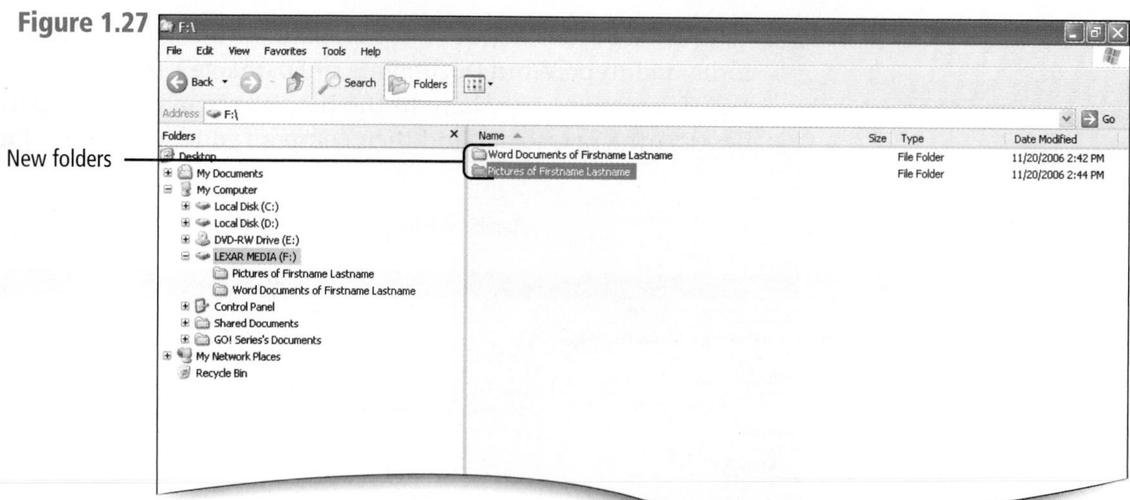

10 In the right pane, click the **Name** column heading several times to sort the folders and file names from *a* to *z* and from *z* to *a*. Notice that the arrow in the Name column heading points up when the folders are displayed in ascending (*a* to *z*) order, and points down when the folders are displayed in descending (*z* to *a*) order. Stop when the folders are sorted in descending alphabetical order—from *z* to *a*—as shown in Figure 1.28.

Figure 1.28

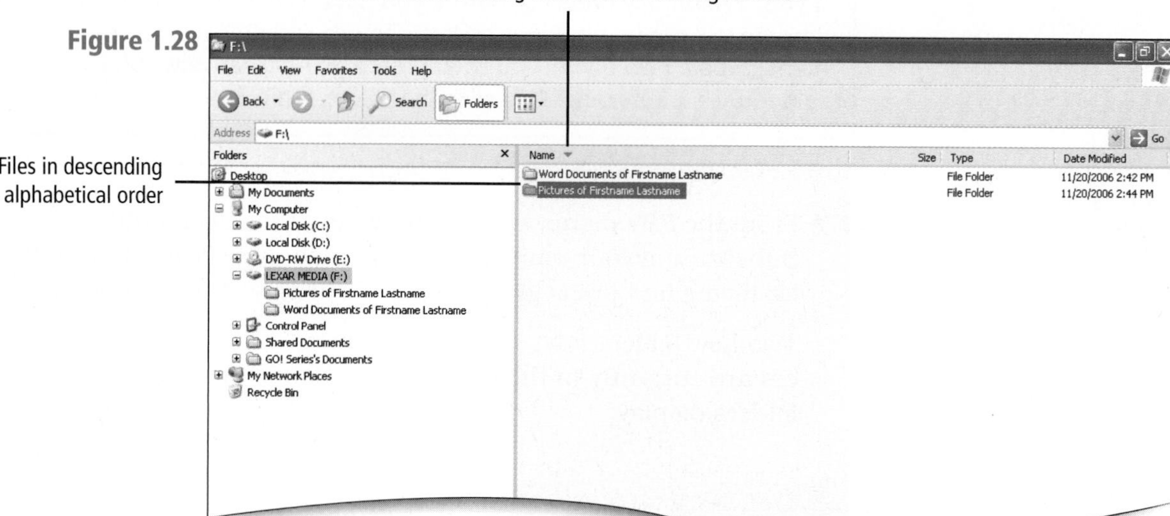

11 In the right pane, move the pointer to the line at the right of the **Name** column heading to display the **resize pointer**, as shown in Figure 1.29.

Figure 1.29

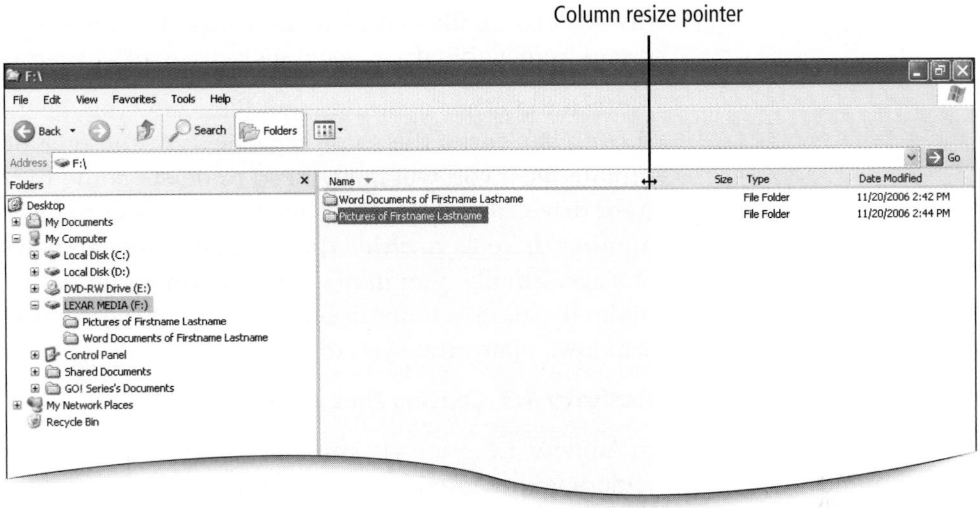

12 Drag the resize pointer to the left about **1 inch**.

The column width is resized. You can resize all the columns in the right pane using the resize pointer.

More Knowledge

Computer Storage Devices

The hard drive (local disk) is usually identified on your computer by the notation C:\ (and sometimes D:\, E:\, and so on for additional drives). A ***floppy disk drive*** provides storage on a floppy disk and is generally identified on your computer by the notation 3 $\frac{1}{2}$ Floppy (A:). Floppy disk drives are becoming outdated—many computers no longer come with a floppy drive. A Zip drive also uses a removable disk that holds more information than a floppy disk. ***Flash drives***—also known as ***USB drives*** or ***thumb drives***—are small storage devices that plug into a computer's Universal Serial Bus (USB) port, a connection between a computer's and a peripheral device such as a printer, a mouse, a keyboard, or a USB drive.

You may also have access to files on another type of storage device, a ***CD-ROM*** disc. CD-ROM stands for Compact Disc-Read Only Memory. If you are using files stored on a CD-ROM, you will need to open a file from the disc, and then save it to a writable drive or copy a file from the CD-ROM disc to another disk and then open it. CD drives can store information on one of two types of CDs—a CD that can be written to but not erased—***CD-R***—or a CD that can be written to and erased many times—***CD-RW***.

Objective 5
Copy, Move, Rename, and Delete Files

Recall that Windows manages your data files because your files are stored on the drives attached to your computer. Copying files from one folder to another is a frequent data management task. For example, you may want to make a backup copy of important information, copy a file from a CD to a local disk, or copy information from your local disk drive to a removable drive. Copying files and folders works the same regardless of the type of drive—removable drive, local disk drive, or shared network drive.

Performing other operations on files, such as deleting them or moving them, also works the same regardless of the type of drive. As you accumulate files, you will likely need to delete some to reduce clutter on your hard drive. You may also want to move documents into other folders on another drive to ***archive*** them—place them somewhere for long-term storage. Finally, you may want to change the names of files or folders to make the names more descriptive. All of these tasks are functions of your Windows operating system.

Activity 1.5 Copying Files and Folders

In Activity 1.5, you will copy files onto your removable drive and into the folders you created in Activity 1.4.

1. Be sure the **My Computer** window is displayed, and that the **Folders** button on the toolbar is selected and the **Folders** task pane is displayed on the left. Place the student CD that came with this book in the CD drive. In the **Folders** task pane, click the **expand button (+)** to the left of the **CD drive** to display the contents of the drive. If a go2007_intro1e dialog box opens, click Cancel.

   The folders and files in the CD drive display, and the expand button changes to a ***collapse button*** (-). Expanded items are in view and collapsed items are hidden from view. The ***expand button*** indicates that additional items are available but hidden from view.

Note — If Your Student Files Are in a Different Location

Some instructors will place the student files in a folder on a shared network drive, or in a file-sharing folder in a course Web site. If you are instructed to use files from another source, follow the instructions below, substituting your file location for the CD drive.

2 In the **Folders** task pane, click the **expand button (+)** to the left of the **go2007_intro1e** folder, click the **expand button (+)** to the left of the **01_student_data_files** folder, and then click the **chapter_01_windowsxp** folder. If necessary, on the Standard Buttons toolbar, click the Views button, and then click Details. Compare your screen with Figure 1.30.

The subfolders in the *chapter_01_windowsxp* folder display in the Folders task pane on the left, and the subfolders and files in the *chapter_01_windowsxp* folder display in the right pane. The files you see may display four letters following the file name, such as *.docx*. These are ***file extensions***, and most files have these extensions—although they may or may not display on your system. Files created by Microsoft Office programs have a standard set of extensions that identify the type of program used to create the file. For example, Microsoft Word documents end in *.doc* or *.docx*, Excel worksheets end in *.xls* or *.xlsx*, PowerPoint presentations end with *.ppt* or *.pptx*, and so on.

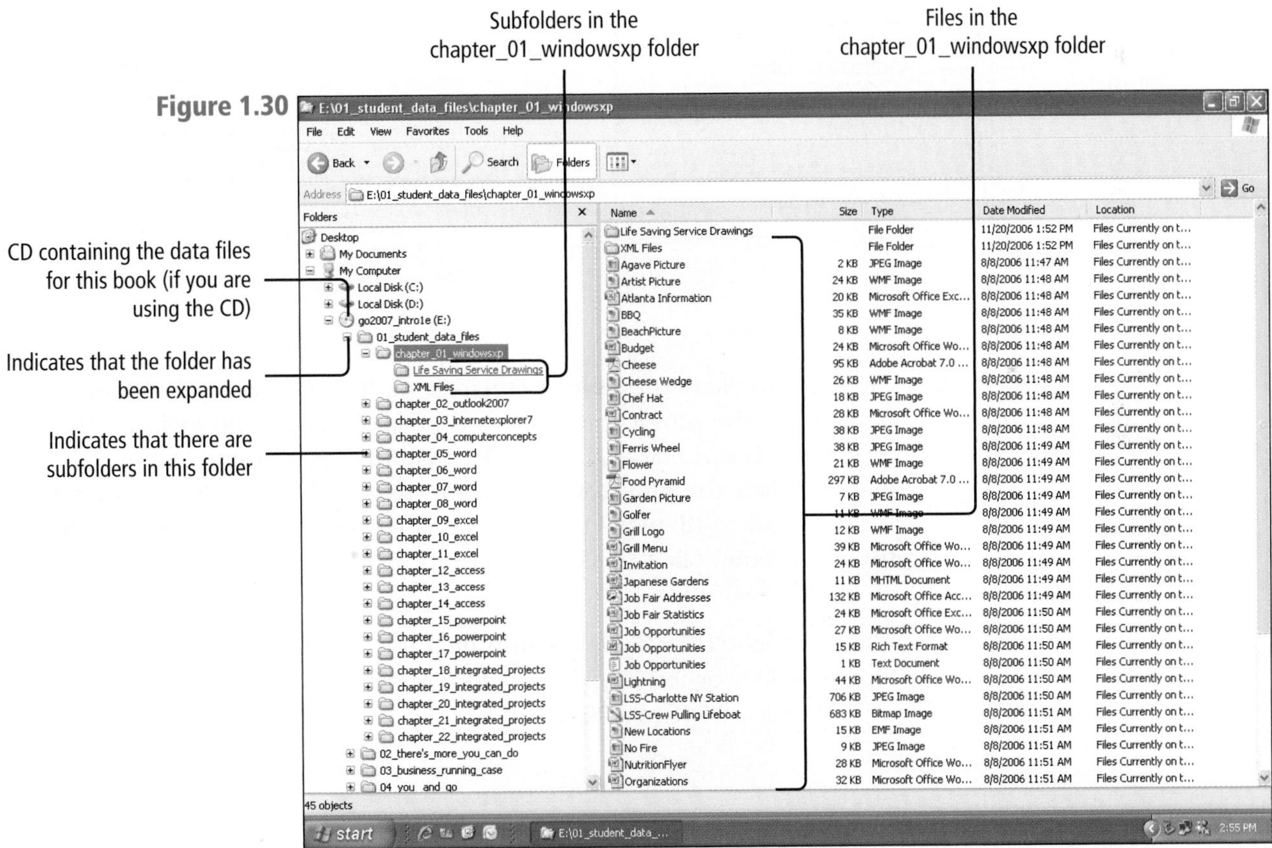

Figure 1.30

3 On the menu bar, click **Tools**, and then from the displayed menu, click **Folder Options**. Near the top of the **Folder Options** dialog box, click the **View tab**. Under **Advanced settings**, locate the **Hide extensions for known file types** check box. If the check box is selected (there is a check mark in it), click to clear the check box, and then compare your screen with Figure 1.31.

In this chapter, from this point on, it is assumed that the file extensions are turned on and will display.

Figure 1.31

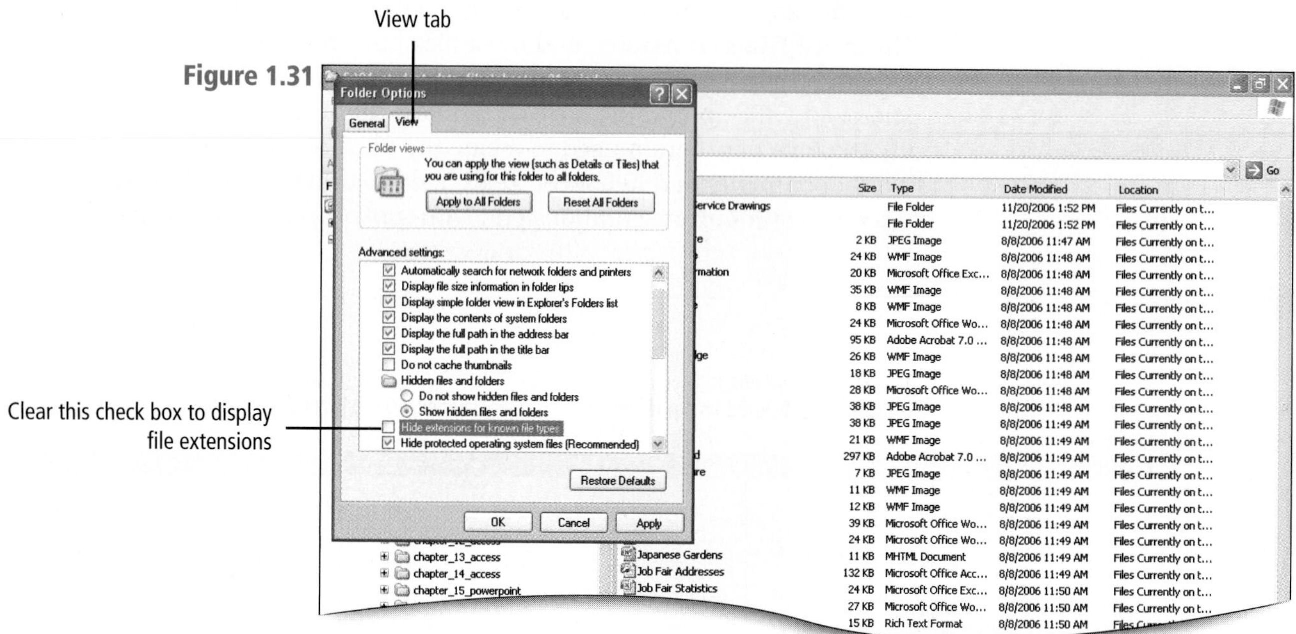

4 Click **OK** to close the **Folder Options** dialog box. In the **Folders** task pane, click the removable drive you used to create the *Pictures of Firstname Lastname* and *Word Documents of Firstname Lastname* folders. Click the **chapter_01_windowsxp** folder, which refreshes the window and re-displays the file names with their file extensions. In the right pane, click the **Type** column heading. Be sure you can see all of the WMF files.

When you click the Type column heading, the files display by file type in *a*-to-*z* order. The displayed WMF files are images that come with Microsoft Office 2007.

5. In the **Name** column, click to select the **Flower.wmf** file. In the **Folders** task pane, scroll as necessary until you can see your removable drive. Watch the shape of the pointer and begin to drag the **Flower.wmf** file over to the **Pictures of Firstname Lastname** folder that you created on your removable drive.

   The Pictures folder on your removable drive is selected, and the file name is attached to the pointer, as shown in Figure 1.32. When you release the mouse button, the file will be copied. Files are copied when dragged to a different drive, and moved when dragged to a different location in the same drive.

6. Release the mouse button to copy the file to the **Pictures of Firstname Lastname** folder.

7. In the **Name** column, click to select the **Plant.wmf** file. From the **Edit** menu, click **Copy**.

   The file is copied to a temporary storage area called the ***Clipboard***. The Clipboard stores the most recent item that was copied.

Figure 1.32

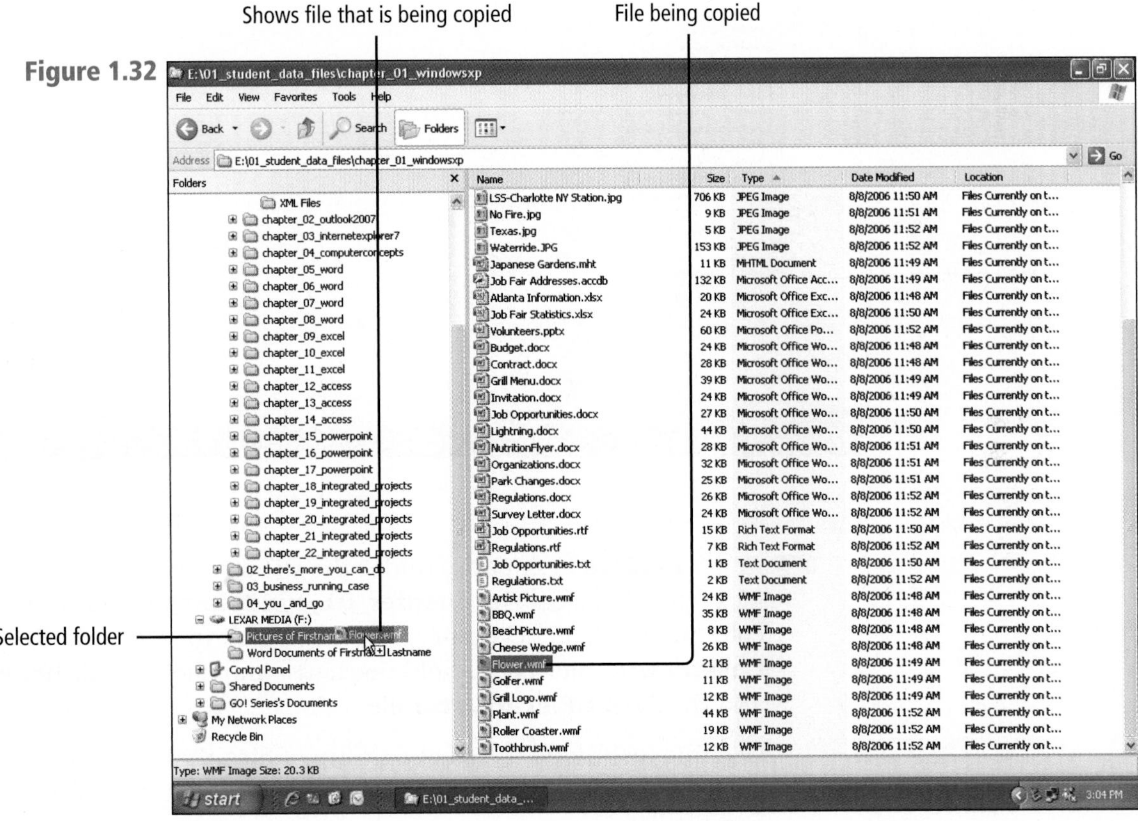

8 In the **Folders** task pane, click to select the **Pictures of Firstname Lastname** folder. From the **Edit** menu, click **Paste**. Compare your screen to Figure 1.33.

The file is copied to the selected folder, and the folder contains two files—the file you dragged to the folder and the file you pasted into the folder. You can see that there are various ways in which you can copy a file from one location to another.

Figure 1.33

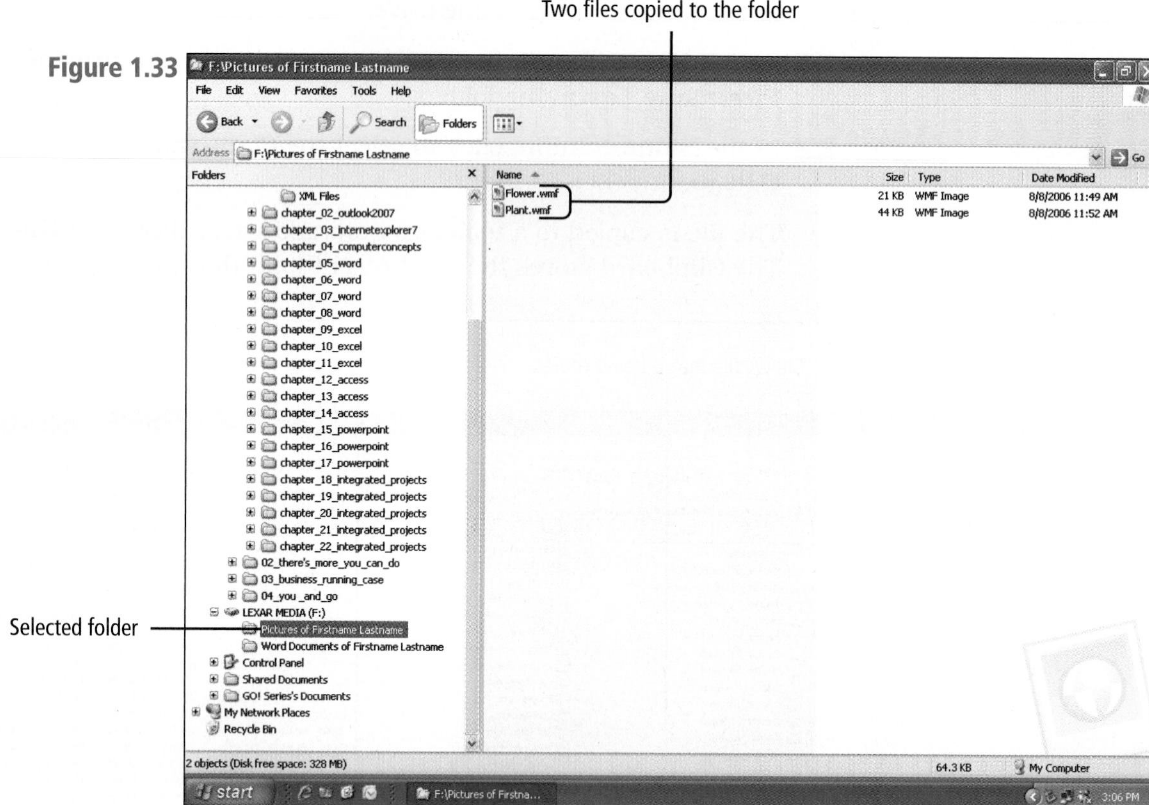

9 In the **Folders** task pane, under the **CD** containing your student files, click to select the **chapter_01_windowsxp** folder. In the **Name** column, scroll as necessary, and then click to select the **Roller Coaster.wmf** file. Then, hold down Ctrl and click the **Golfer.wmf** file and the **Artist Picture.wmf** file.

Use this technique to select a group of files that are not adjacent to (next to) each other. This technique works in all Windows programs and file lists.

10 From the **File** menu, point to **Send To**, and then click the name of your removable disk drive.

The files are copied to your removable drive. This copy option enables you to send a file or files to the drive of your choice, but does not permit you to specify a folder on that drive.

11 In the right pane, click the **Name** column heading, and then scroll to the top of the list of folders and files. In the **Folders** task pane, scroll down if necessary to see your removable drive. Drag the **XML Files** folder over the name of your removable drive until it is selected, and then release the mouse button. Compare your screen with Figure 1.34.

The folder and all of the files in the folder are copied to your removable drive.

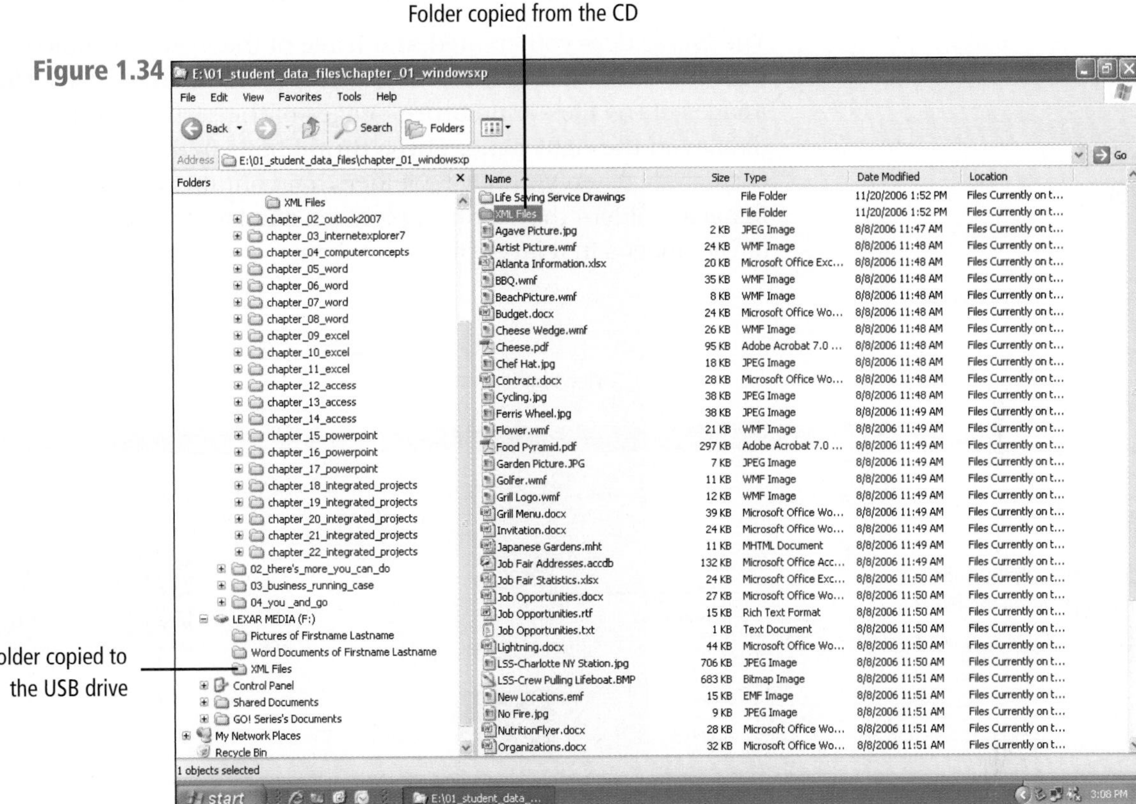

Figure 1.34

Activity 1.6 Moving, Renaming, and Deleting Files

In Activity 1.6, you will move files from one location on your removable drive to another location on the same drive. You will also rename and delete files.

1 In the **Folders** task pane, scroll down if necessary and then click the removable drive you are using to store your files. In the right pane, click the **Name** column as necessary to display the files in alphabetical order. Click the **Views button arrow** and then click **Thumbnails**. Compare your screen with Figure 1.35.

The two folders you created and three of the files you copied—along with the XML Files folder—display in the right pane. Small ***thumbnail*** images of the files—miniature images of the pictures in the files—display in the right pane. These thumbnails make it easy to select the correct file when you have a folder that contains a large number of images. Folders that contain pictures display thumbnails of up to four of the images in a large file folder icon.

Figure 1.35

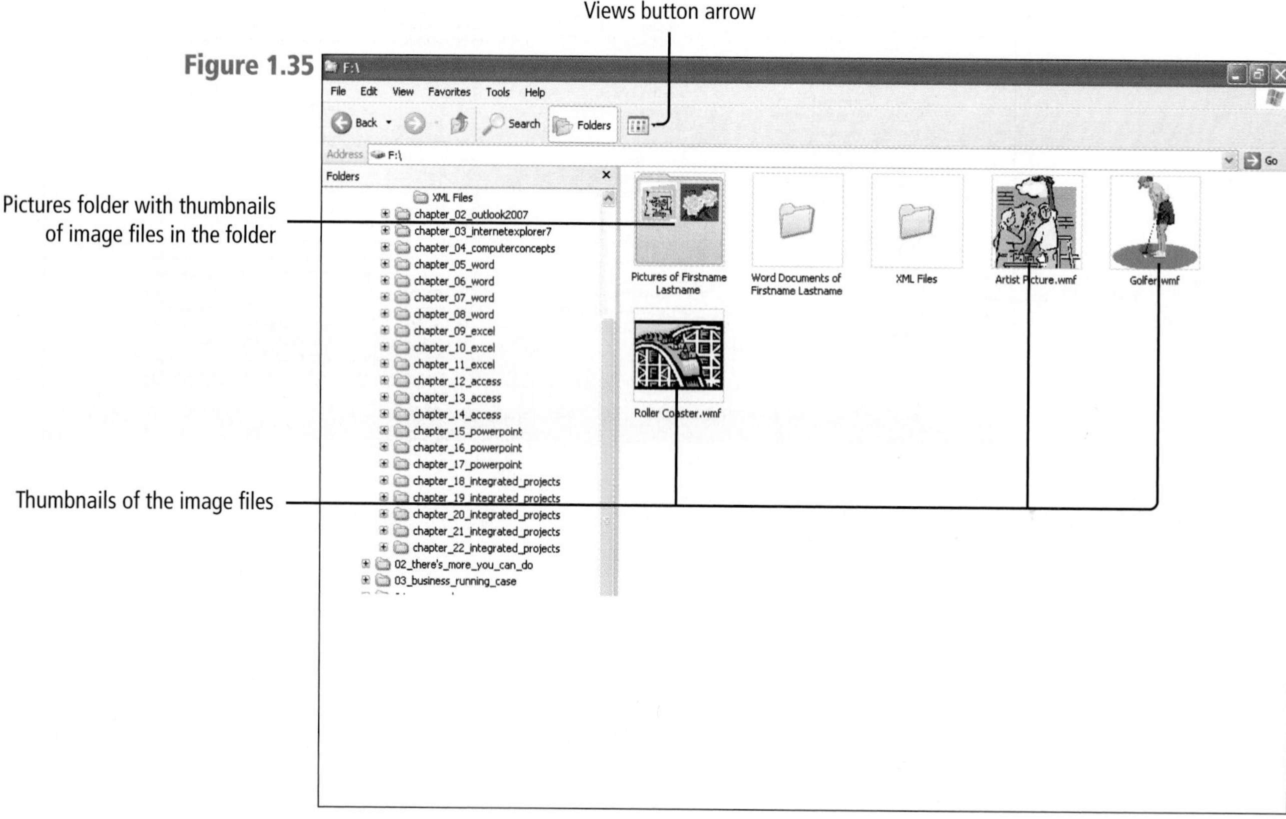

2. In the right pane, click the **Artist Picture.wmf** file. Hold down the mouse button, drag the file to the **Pictures of Firstname Lastname** folder that you created, and then release the mouse button.

   When you drag a file from one folder to another in the same drive, the file is moved, rather than copied.

3. Drag the **Golfer.wmf** file to the **Pictures** folder, and then drag the **Roller Coaster.wmf** file to the **Pictures** folder.

4. In the **Folders** task pane, click the **Pictures of Firstname Lastname** folder in your removable drive. On the Standard Buttons toolbar, click the **Views** button, and then click **Thumbnails**. Compare your screen with Figure 1.36.

Figure 1.36

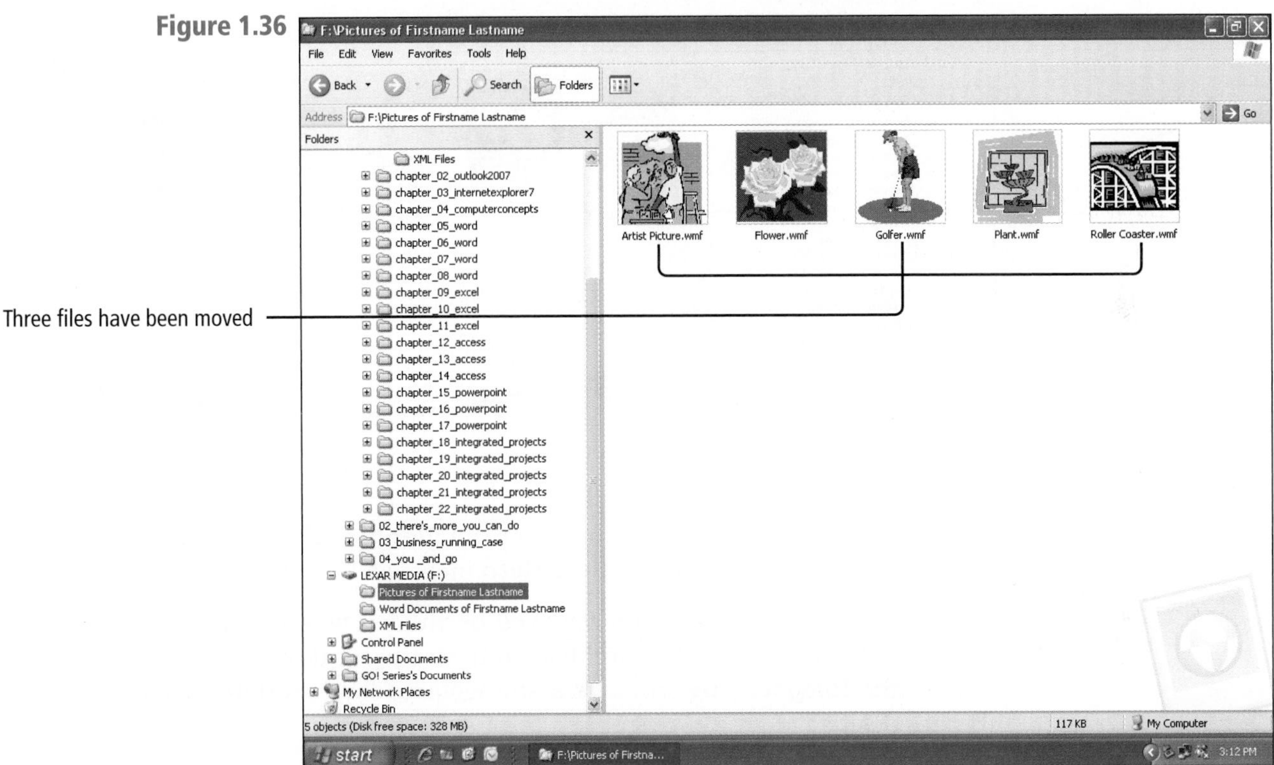

5 In the right pane, right-click the **Flower.wmf** file. Then, from the displayed shortcut menu, click the **Rename** command. Click to position the insertion point at the beginning of the file name, type **Water** and then press Spacebar. Press Enter to change the file name to *Water Flower.wmf*. Compare your screen with Figure 1.37.

When the file extensions are displayed, you need to include the extension when you rename the file. There are several restrictions for naming files or folders. A file name can contain up to 255 characters, including spaces, although the file name cannot begin with a space. It also cannot contain the following characters: \ / : * ? " < > |

Figure 1.37

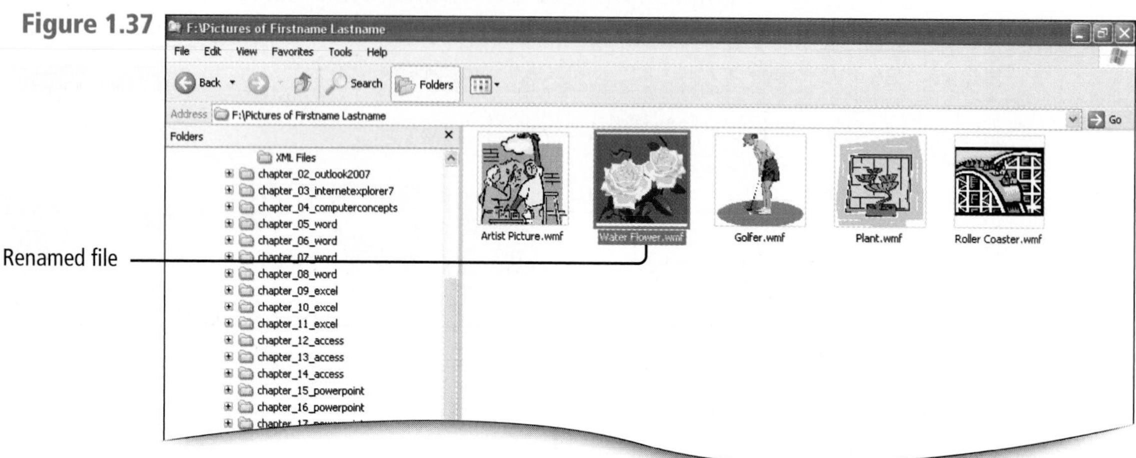

6 In the right pane, click to select the **Plant.wmf** file, and then press Delete. In the **Confirm File Delete** message box, click **Yes**.

The file is permanently removed because it was stored on a removable drive. Files that are deleted from the hard drive are moved to the ***Recycle Bin***, which is a storage area for files that have been deleted.

Note — If You Cannot Delete a File

Sometimes you will try to delete a file and a message displays indicating that the file cannot be deleted. This usually means that the file is open. You must close a file before you can delete it.

7 In the **Folders** task pane, click to select your removable disk. In the right pane, select the **XML Files** folder, and then press Delete.

8 In the **Confirm Folder Delete** dialog box, click **Yes** to delete the folder.

The folder and all of the files and folders it contains are deleted.

More Knowledge

Recovering Deleted Files

If you accidentally delete a file from the hard disk drive that you want to keep, there is a good chance you can recover it. Windows temporarily stores files deleted from your hard drive in a Recycle Bin, which you can find on the desktop or in the My Computer Folders pane. You can open the Recycle Bin in the same way you open a file folder. If the discarded files have not been permanently removed, right-click the file name in the Contents pane, and then click Restore in the shortcut menu.

Activity 1.7 Capturing an Image of a Screen

Windows includes a screen capture utility that enables you to capture an image of your screen and then print it or save it as a file.

1 On your keyboard, locate and press PrtScr.

The Print Screen key on your keyboard is commonly located near the right side of the top row of keys. This key captures an image of the entire screen and places it in a temporary storage area called the Clipboard. Items in the Clipboard can be placed in a document using the Paste command.

2 Click the **Start** button start, point to **All Programs**, point to **Accessories**, and then click **WordPad**. If necessary, maximize the WordPad window.

WordPad is a simple word-processing program that comes with Windows XP.

3 In the WordPad window, type **Firstname Lastname** using your own name. Press Enter two times.

4 From the WordPad menu bar, click **Edit**, and then click **Paste**. Compare your screen with Figure 1.38.

The captured screen is pasted at the insertion point. The image is larger than the WordPad page.

Figure 1.38

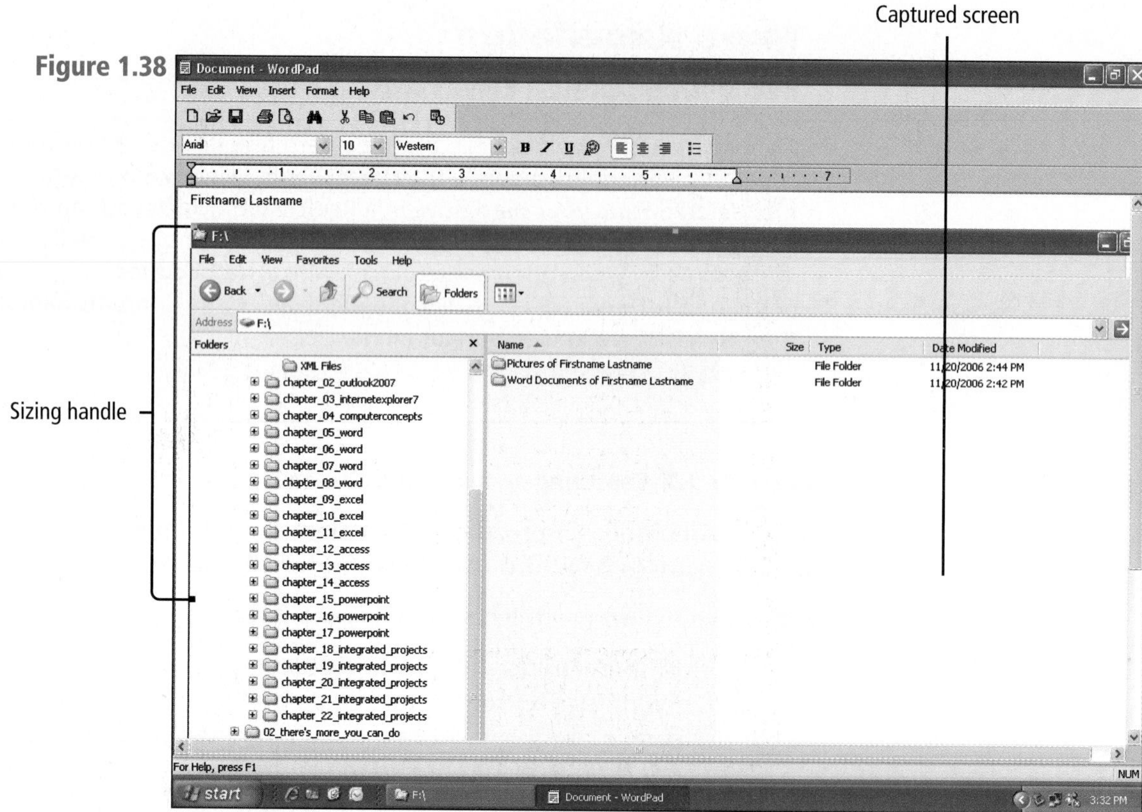

5 If necessary, use the vertical and horizontal scroll bars to display the sizing handle in the lower right corner of the pasted image. In the lower right corner of the image, move the pointer over the sizing handle—the little box in the corner—to display the diagonal resize pointer ⤡.

When an image is selected, ***sizing handles*** display in all four corners and in the middle of the side and top borders. Use handles to resize the image in a manner similar to the way you resized a window.

6 With the diagonal size pointer, drag up and to the left of **6 inches** on the ruler. Compare your screen with Figure 1.39.

Recall that to drag an object, you need to point, click, and move the mouse to the desired location. Use the ruler as a guide.

Six inches mark

Diagonal resize pointer

Figure 1.39

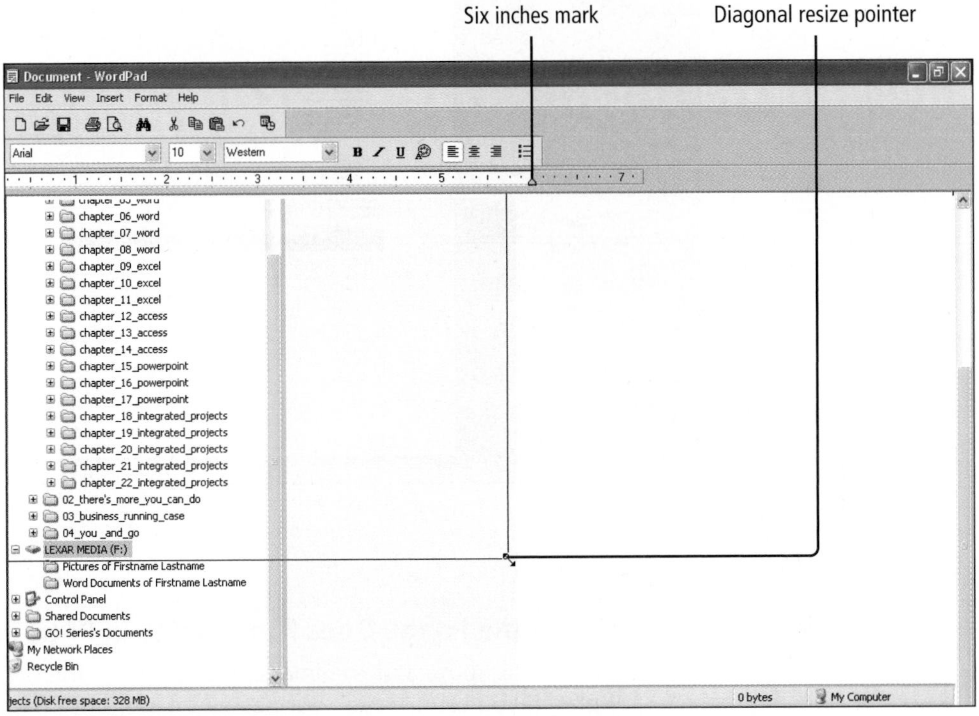

7 Release the mouse button, and then from the File menu click **Print Preview** to display the Print Preview window. Compare your screen to Figure 1.40.

8 In the **Print Preview** title bar, click the **Close** button. Alternatively, click the **Close** button on the Print Preview toolbar.

9 Check your Course Syllabus or Chapter Assignment Sheet, or ask your instructor, to determine if you are to submit a printed or electronic copy of this file. To print, from the WordPad toolbar, click the **Print** button. To submit electronically using your college's course management system, consult your instructor's directions for saving and submitting the file.

10 From the **File** menu, click **Exit**. When prompted to save your work, click **No**.

Figure 1.40

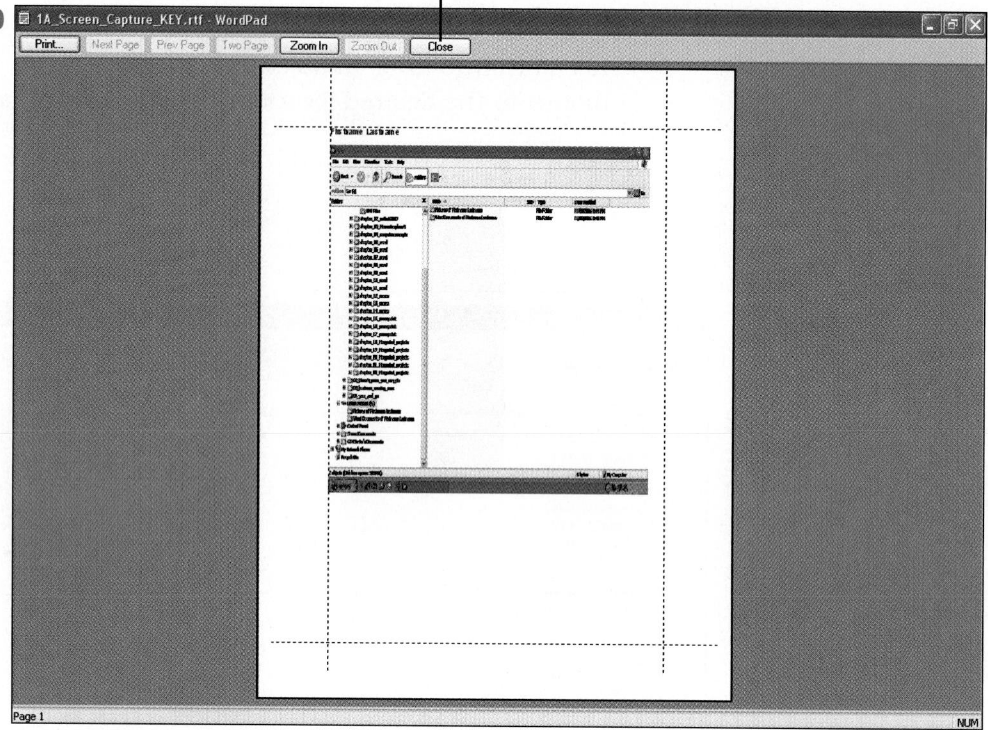

Alert!

What If the Image Does Not Display in Print Preview?

On some computers, if the image is larger than the page, the image will not display. If you cannot see your pasted image, close the Print Preview window and use the sizing handle to reduce the size of the image again. Repeat this procedure until you can see the image in Print Preview.

Objective 6
Find Files and Folders

As you use a computer, you will likely accumulate a large number of files and folders. It's easy to forget where you stored a file, or what you named it. Windows XP provides a search function that enables you to find files and folders.

Activity 1.8 Finding Files and Folders

In Activity 1.8, you will use several different methods to search for files and folders.

1 In the **Folders** task pane, click **My Computer**. On the Standard Buttons toolbar, click the **Search** button [Search], and then compare your screen with Figure 1.41.

The Search Companion task pane displays on the left. Here you can search for specific file types or you can search through all the files and folders.

Figure 1.41

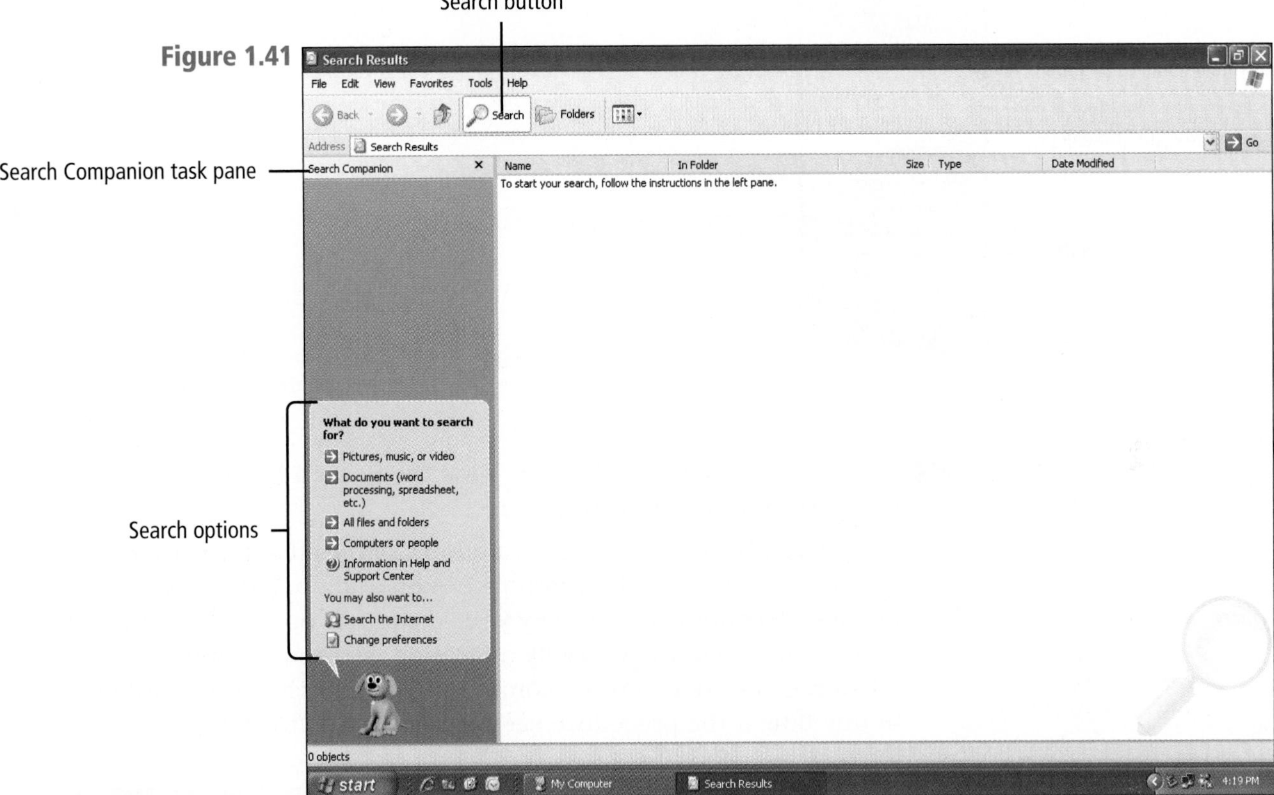

Alert!

What If Windows Desktop Search starts instead of the Search Companion?

At the bottom of the Windows Desktop Search pane, click the link to the Search Companion. Maximize the Search Results window and complete the rest of Activity 1.8 as directed. When you are done with Activity 1.8, close both the Search Results window and the Windows Desktop Search pane.

2 In the **Search Companion** task pane, click the **All files and folders** option.

A search dialog box displays. Here you can specify the file name (or part of a file name) or text contained in the file. You can also narrow the search by specifying the search location.

3 In the **All or part of the file name** box, type **coaster**. If necessary, click the **Look in down arrow**, and then click **My Computer**. Compare your screen with Figure 1.42.

The actual file name is capitalized, but this search option is not case sensitive.

Figure 1.42

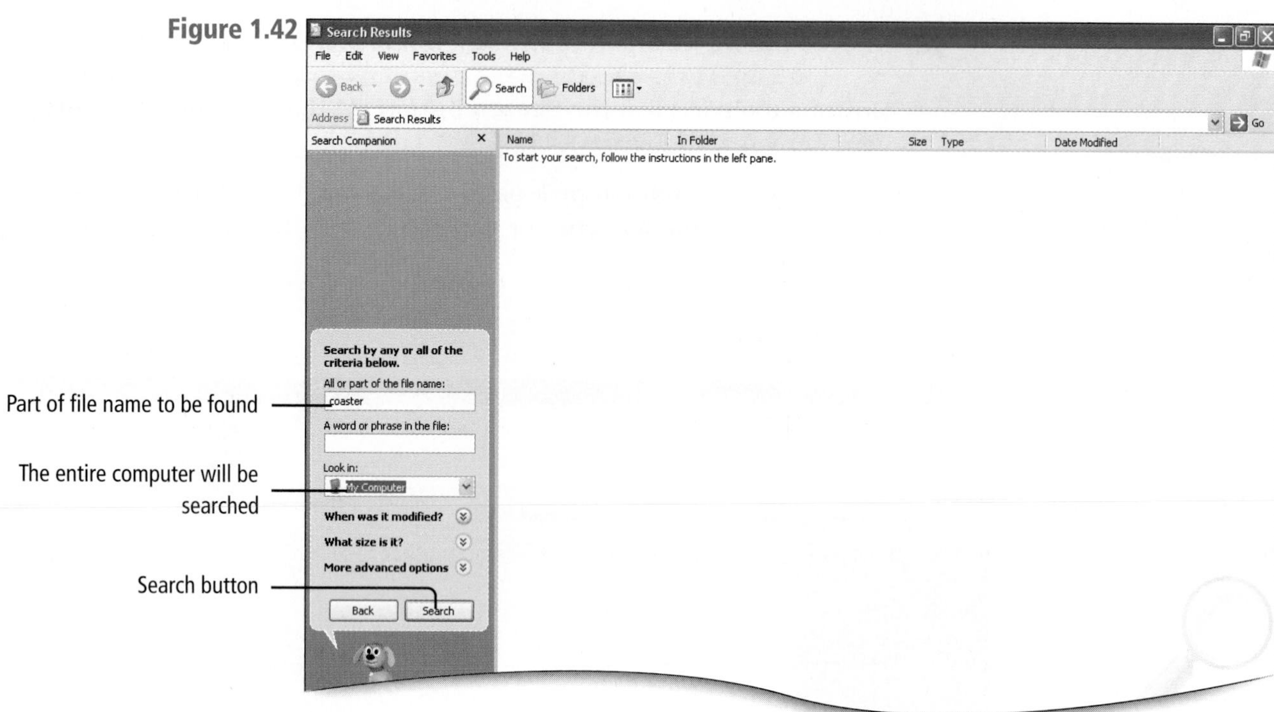

4 At the bottom of the task pane, click the **Search** button, and then compare your screen with Figure 1.43.

The search begins. Notice that a couple of files display rather quickly, but the search program goes on and on. (You may see only one file, depending on the way your computer has been set up.) This is because you did not specify a location, so the program is checking all storage locations on the computer. You can click the Stop button at any time if the procedure seems to be taking too long.

Figure 1.43

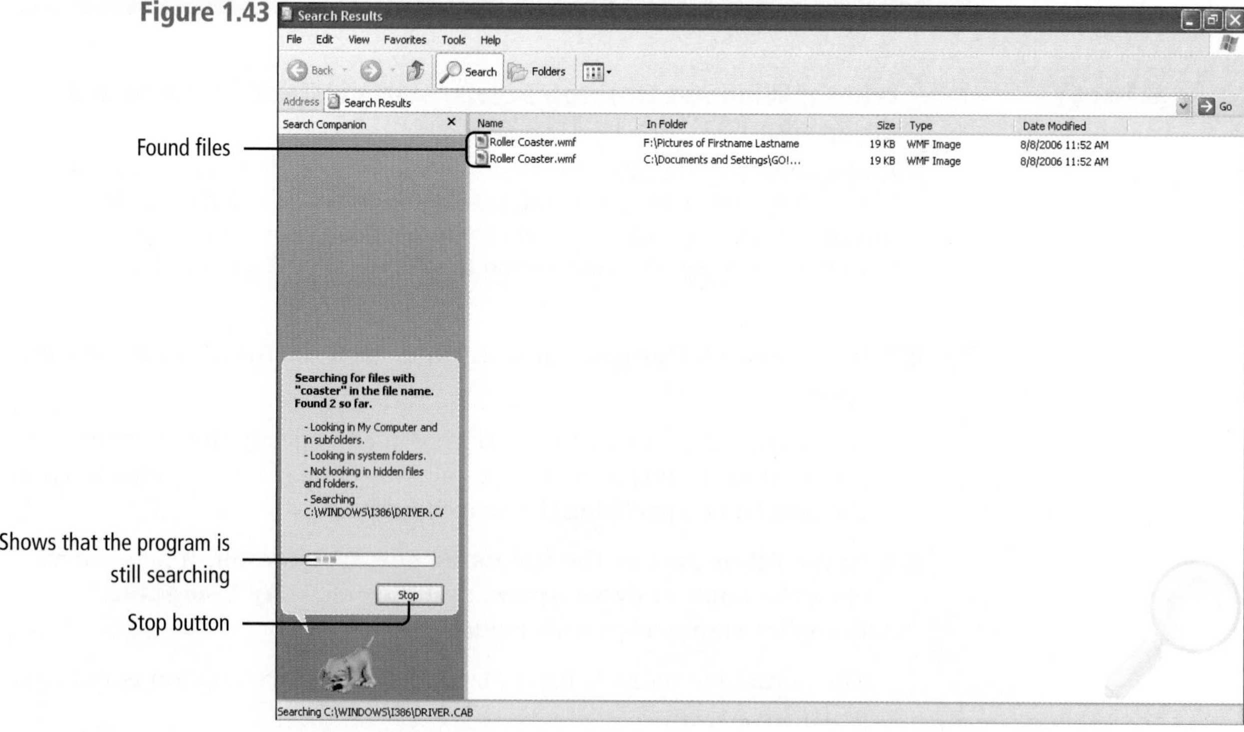

5 Click **Stop** to stop the current search. Click **Start a new search**, and then click **Pictures, music, or video**. Click to select the **Pictures and Photos** check box. In the **All or part of the file name** box, type **surf**

This is part of several file names in the Life Saving Service Drawings folder on your student CD.

6 In the **Search Companion** task pane, click the **Use advanced search options** check box to add more search options. At the right of the **Look in** box, click the arrow. From the location list, click your student **CD** and then compare your screen with Figure 1.44. If you are not using the CD, select the location where your student files are stored.

Figure 1.44

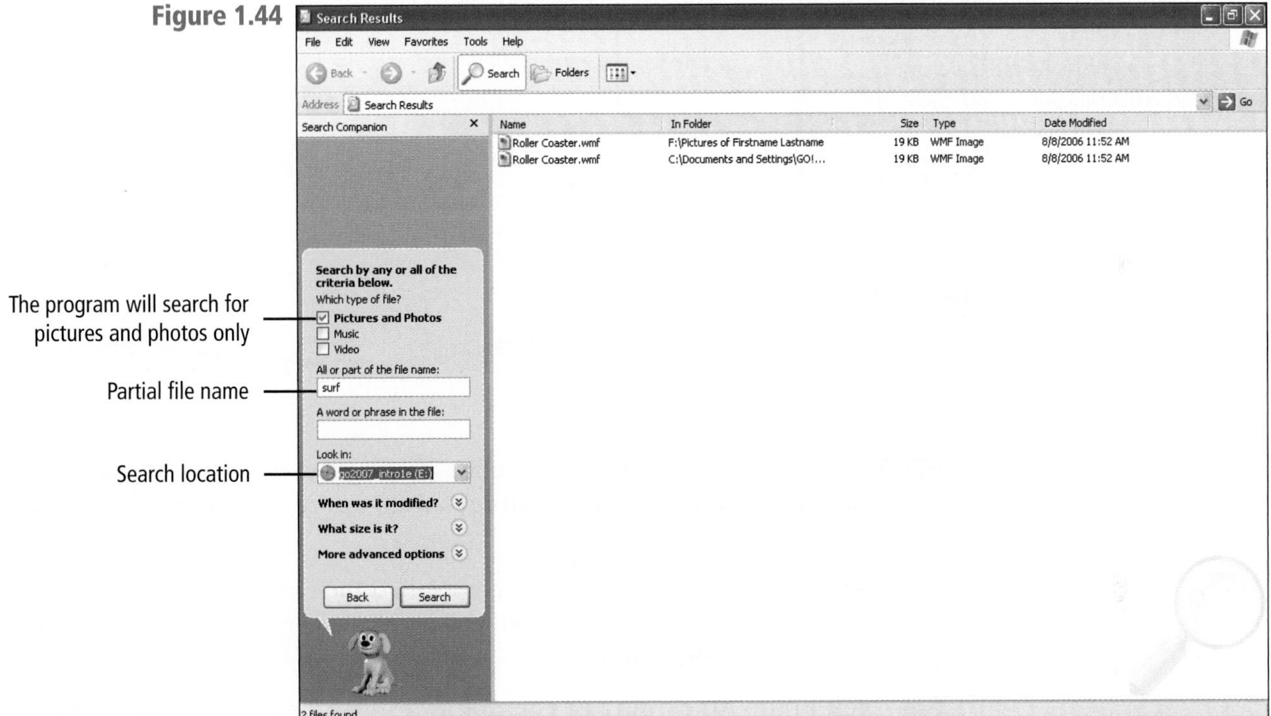

7 At the bottom of the task pane, click the **Search** button. Compare your screen with Figure 1.45.

Three files are found. This time, the search only took a few seconds.

Figure 1.45

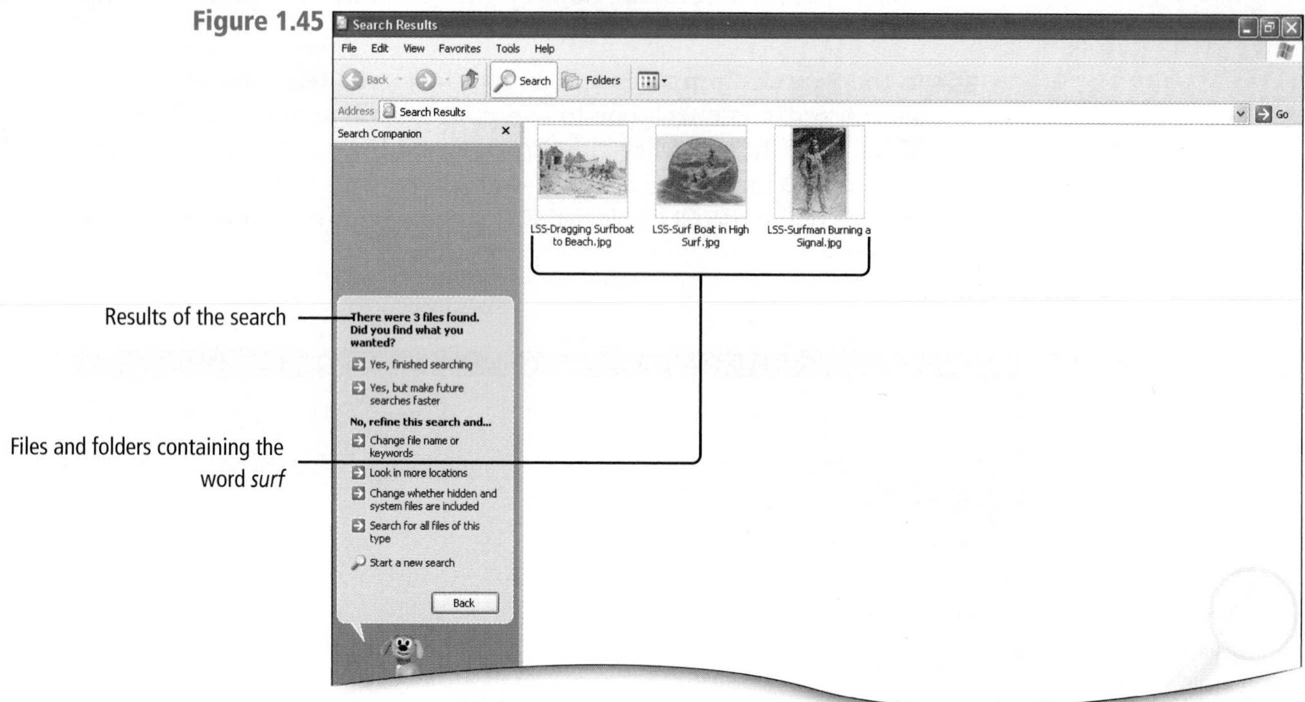

8 Scroll down, if necessary, and click the **Start a new search** option. Click the **Documents (word processing, spreadsheet, etc.)** option.

This dialog box gives you greater control over the search. You can search for documents that have specified file extensions, or you can search for documents last modified during a certain time period. You can even combine the two.

9 Click in the **All or part of the document name** box and type ***.docx** Click the **Use advanced search options** check box to add more search options. At the right of the **Look in** box, click the arrow. From the location list, click your student **CD** or other student file location. Click the **Search** button and view the results.

This restricts the search to Word 2007 documents, which have the .docx extension. The asterisk is called a ***wildcard*** and means that you will be searching for anything that has the *.docx* extension. This is very helpful when you cannot remember the file name or where you put it.

10 In the **Search Companion** task pane, click the **Look in arrow** again, and then click **Local Disk (C:)**—or **Local Hard Drives**. Click the **Search** button. Compare your screen with Figure 1.46.

The right pane displays the files that have the *.docx* extension. The list may be quite long.

11 On the **Search Companion** task pane, click the **Stop** button.

Figure 1.46

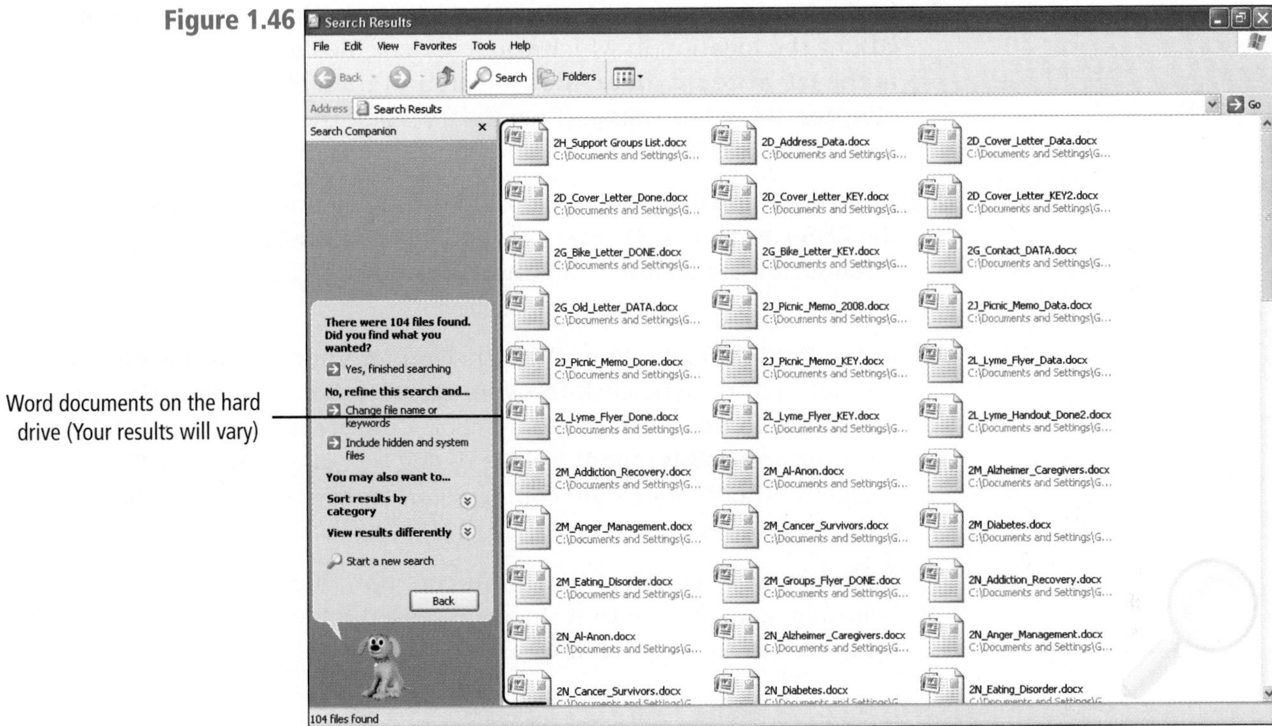

Objective 7
Compress Files

Some files may be too large to send quickly as an e-mail attachment. For example, files containing graphics tend to be quite large. Windows XP includes a feature with which you can ***compress***—reduce the file size of—one or more files into a single file that uses a *.zip* file extension. These files can then be unzipped for editing on any other computer running Windows XP.

Activity 1.9 Compressing Files

In Activity 1.9, you will compress a single file and then compress several files at the same time.

1 On the Standard Buttons toolbar, click the **Folders** button. In the Folders task pane, click **My Computer**.

Note — To Work with Third-Party Zip Programs

If you are using a third-party zip program, such as WinZip™ or PKZIP™, you will need to use that program to complete this task—the procedure listed below will not work.

2 In the **Folders** task pane, click the drive containing your student **CD**, or the location in which your student files are stored. Navigate to the **01_student_data_files** folder, and then click **chapter_01_windowsxp**. If necessary, click the **Views** button, and then click **Details**.

3 Click the **Lightning.docx** file. Hold down Ctrl and then click to select the **LSS-Charlotte NY Station.jpg** file, the **LSS-Crew Pulling Lifeboat.bmp** file, and the **Volunteers.pptx** file. Drag these four files to copy them to your removable drive.

4 In the **Folders** task pane, click the icon for your removable disk. In the right pane, right-click the **Volunteers.pptx** file. Notice the file size. Point to **Send To**, and then click **Compressed (zipped) Folder**. If a **Compressed (zipped) Folder** dialog box displays, click **Yes** to designate the Windows XP compression feature to zip your file. Compare your screen with Figure 1.47.

A compressed version of the Volunteers.pptx file displays as Volunteers.zip. Notice that the compressed folder is reduced in size compared to the original file.

Figure 1.47

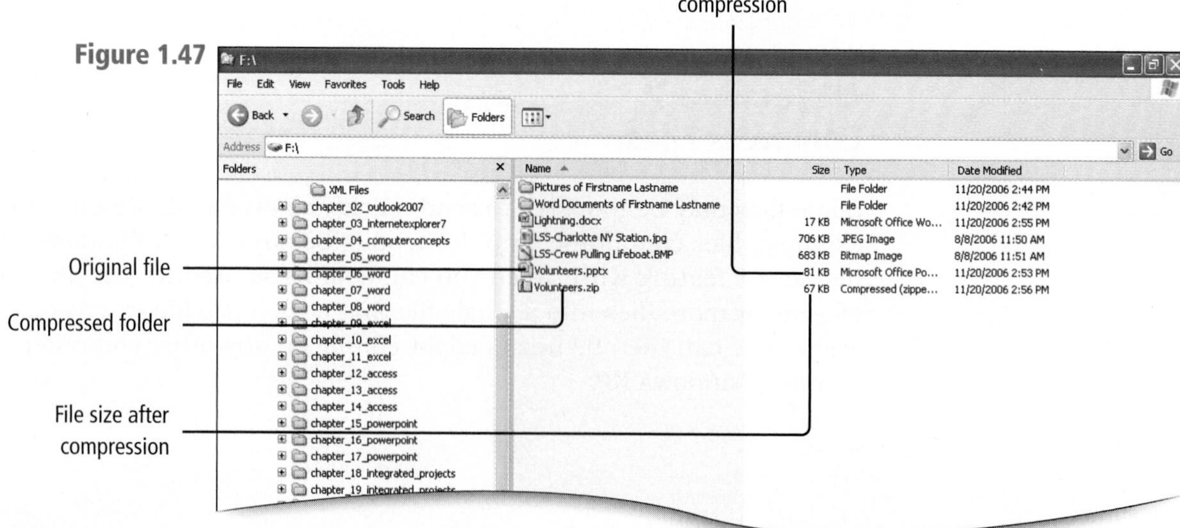

5 Repeat the procedure you used in Step 4 to compress the other three files you just copied to your removable drive—**Lightning.docx**, **LSS-Charlotte NY Station.jpg**, and **LSS-Crew Pulling Lifeboat.bmp**. Compare your screen with Figure 1.48.

Notice that the amount of compression depends on the type of file being compressed. Word files can often be reduced by 10 to 20 percent, while files that use compression features when the files are saved—such as *.jpg* or *.pdf* files—do not benefit much from further compression.

Figure 1.48

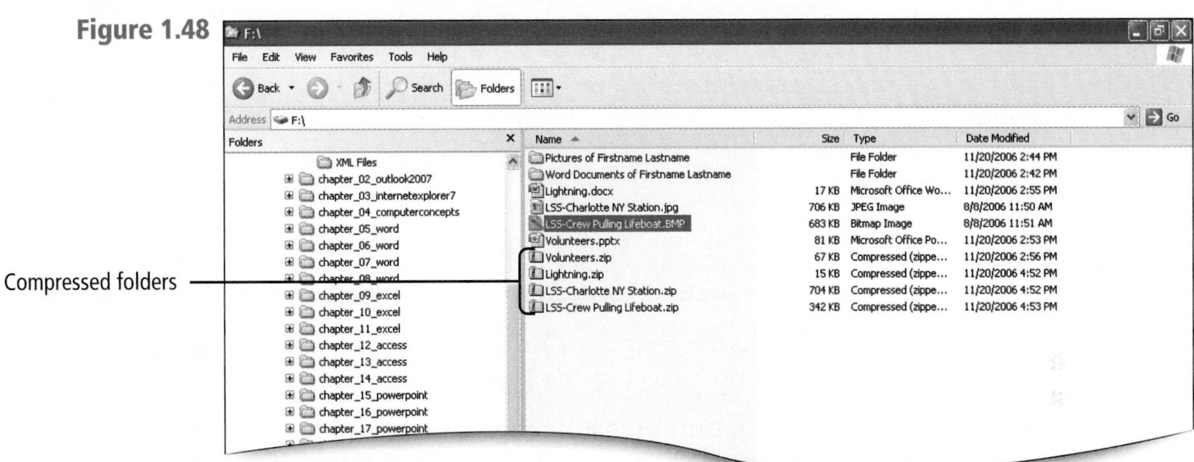

6 Click the **Lightning.docx** file. Hold down Ctrl and then click to select the **LSS-Charlotte NY Station.jpg** file, the **LSS-Crew Pulling Lifeboat.bmp** file, and the **Volunteers.pptx** file. Press Delete to remove the original files, and then click **Yes** when prompted.

7 In the **Folders** task pane, click the **Pictures of Firstname Lastname** folder. From the **Edit** menu, click **Select All** to select all the files in the folder. Alternatively, hold down Ctrl and press A.

8 Right-click the **Artist Picture.wmf** file, click **Send To**, and then click **Compressed (zipped) Folder**.

All four files are compressed into one folder, called *Artist Picture.zip*. The compressed folder takes the name of whichever file you right-click when you compress more than one file at a time.

9. Double-click the **Artist Picture.zip** folder to display the contents of the compressed folder. Compare your screen with Figure 1.49.

Figure 1.49

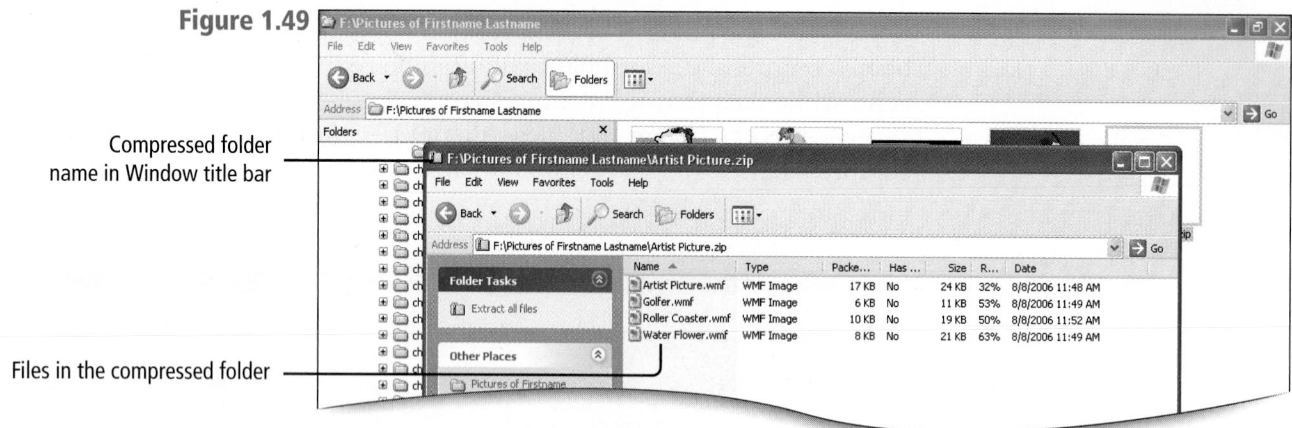

10. In the **Artist Picture.zip** window title bar, click the **Close** button [X]. In the Standard Buttons toolbar, click the **Up** button [Up] to move up a level in the **Folders** task pane.

    The Up button is a handy way to move up in the Windows folder hierarchy—each time you click the button, you move up one folder level.

11. Double-click the **Lightning.zip** compressed folder. In the left pane, click **Extract all files** to start the Extraction Wizard. Compare your screen with Figure 1.50.

Figure 1.50

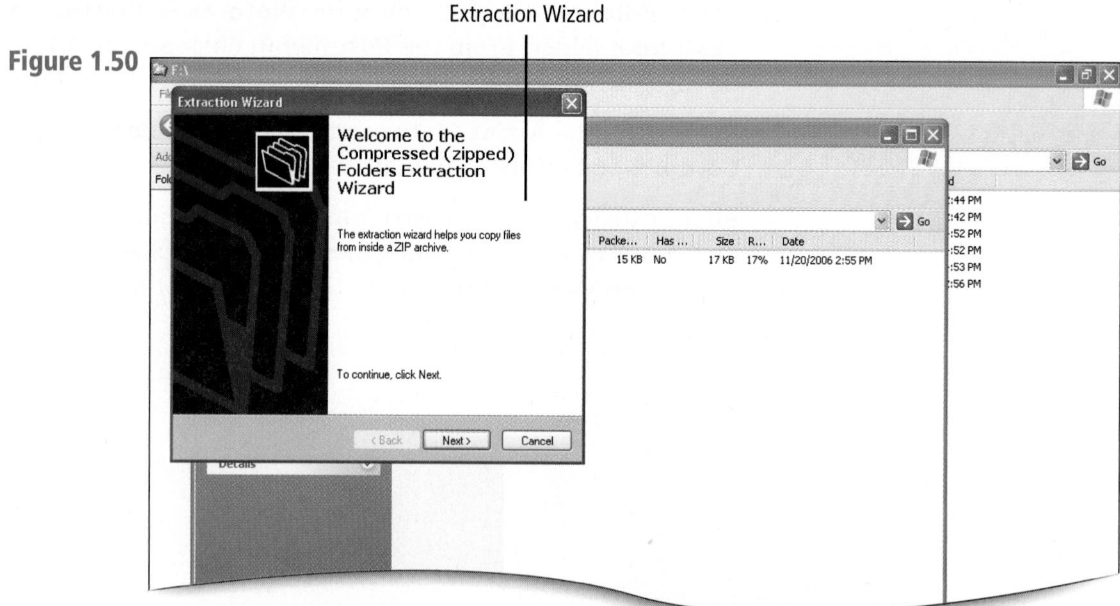

12 Click **Next** to display the second **Extraction Wizard** dialog box, which enables you to change the location of the file.

If you do not change the file location, the file will be extracted to the folder that contains the zipped file.

13 In the **Extraction Wizard** dialog box, click the **Next** button to accept the default location.

14 In the **Extraction Wizard** dialog box, clear the **Show extracted files** check box, and then click **Finish**. Close the Lightning.zip window.

The Show extracted files option is useful when you are sending files to a different location and want to move to that location when the Extraction Wizard closes.

The file is extracted and placed in a folder along with the compressed file, as shown in Figure 1.51.

Figure 1.51

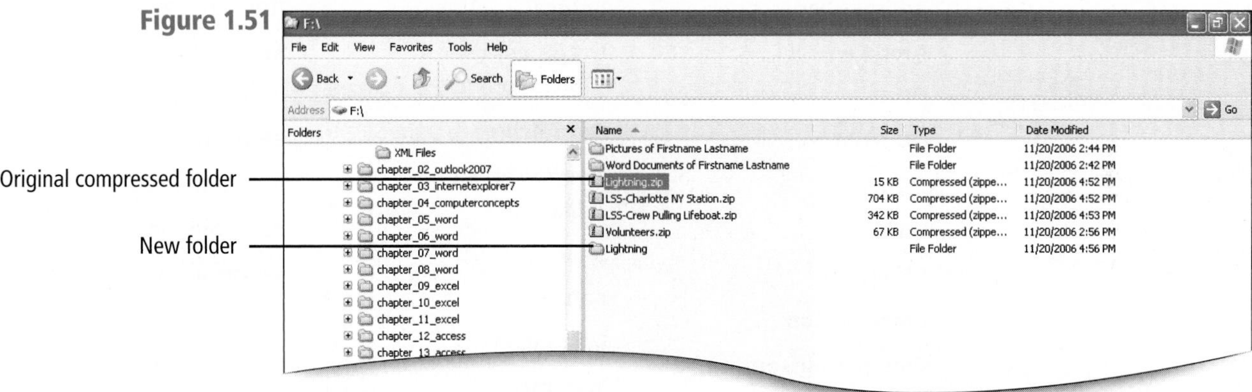

15 On the menu bar, click **Tools**, and then from the displayed menu, click **Folder Options**. Near the top of the **Folder Options** dialog box, click the **View tab**. Under **Advanced settings**, locate the **Hide extensions for known file types** check box. Click to select the check box. Click **OK** to turn off the file extensions.

16 Close the **Removable Media** window.

More Knowledge

File Associations and Compression Programs

You may see a dialog box when you click the Compressed (zipped) Folder command. Because every file type needs to be associated with a program, your computer may already associate files that have the *.zip* extension with a third-party program such as WinZip. The dialog box will ask whether you want to designate Compressed (zipped) Folders as the program for handling ZIP files (compressed files that have a *.zip* extension). If you are working in a lab, ask the lab manager how to answer this question. If you are working at home, click Yes, unless you want to use another program to compress your files.

Content-Based Assessments

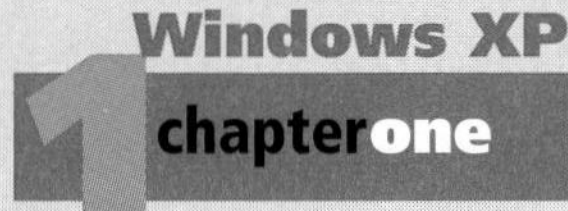

Summary

You will find that a working knowledge of Windows functions is useful as you create files in various programs like those in Microsoft Office. In this chapter, you practiced setting up, organizing, and navigating the Windows desktop. You adjusted window size and moved windows. You created folders to store your documents and then copied, moved, renamed, and deleted files. Finally, you compressed files to save space.

Key Terms

Content-Based Assessments

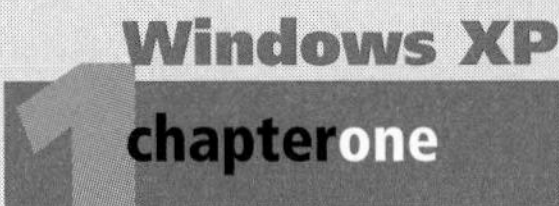

Matching

Match each term in the second column with its correct definition in the first column. Write the letter of the term on the blank line in front of the correct definition.

____ **1.** A bar that contains the Start button, buttons representing open programs, and other buttons that will activate programs.

____ **2.** The arrow, I-beam, or other symbol that moves when you move the mouse or other pointing device, and that indicates a location or position on your screen.

____ **3.** A box that displays information and usually consists of a title bar, menu bar, status bar, and toolbars, and that always has a Minimize button.

____ **4.** The area at the top of a window that displays the file name and also contains the Minimize, Maximize/Restore Down, and Close buttons.

____ **5.** A list of context-sensitive commands—commands that are commonly used when working on the selected object—usually activated by right-clicking a screen item.

____ **6.** An area to the right of the Start button that contains shortcut icons for commonly used programs.

____ **7.** The area on the right side of the taskbar where the clock and system notifications display, and where notifications display that keep you informed about processes that are occurring in the background, such as antivirus software checking, network connections, and other utility programs.

____ **8.** A horizontal bar at the bottom of the document window that provides information about the current state of what you are viewing in the window, for example the page number of a document.

____ **9.** The Windows feature that enables you to view text that extends beyond the edges of the screen.

____ **10.** A Windows object used to keep related files stored together in one location.

____ **11.** A compact disc that can be used over and over again to read and save files.

____ **12.** The three- or four-letter ending to a file—that may or may not display—and that identifies the file type.

____ **13.** The term given to an asterisk (*) or other character used to substitute for several characters in a file search.

____ **14.** A miniature representation of the contents of a picture file, used in one of the file views in My Computer.

____ **15.** To reduce the size of a file.

A CD-RW
B Compress
C File extension
D Folder
E Mouse pointer
F Notification area
G Quick Launch toolbar
H Scroll bar
I Shortcut menu
J Status bar
K Taskbar
L Thumbnail
M Title bar
N Wildcard
O Window

Content-Based Assessments

Fill in the Blank

Write the correct word in the space provided.

1. A(n) ______________ is a graphic representation that enables you to run a program or use a program function.
2. Windows XP is an example of a(n) ________________, which coordinates the activities of a computer.
3. The ______________ button on the left end of the taskbar is used to run programs, change system settings, or find help.
4. When more than one document or program is open at the same time, you can switch back and forth between them by clicking the appropriate button in the ______________.
5. A(n) ______________ is a second-level menu that is accessed using a menu command.
6. When you delete a file, it is stored in a temporary area called the ______________, from which it can often be recovered.
7. A box that asks you to make a decision about an individual object or topic is called a(n) ______________ box.
8. The arrow, I-beam, or other symbol that shows the location or position of the mouse on your screen is called a mouse ______________.
9. When you right-click an object, a(n) ______________ menu displays.
10. The bar that usually displays under the menu bar, and that uses buttons to activate commands, is call a(n) ______________.
11. To make a window fill the screen, use the ______________ button from the title bar.
12. You can hide a program or document without closing it by clicking the ______________ button.
13. In My Computer, you can sort file names alphabetically by clicking the ______________ column heading.

Fill in the Blank

14. The main storage device on your computer is the _____________ disk drive.

15. A file _____________, which consists of the last three or four characters of a file name, indicates which program was used to create the file.

Glossary

Active window The window in which the mouse pointer movements, commands, or text entry occur when two or more windows are open.

Address bar Displays the path of the current file or folder; also, in Internet Explorer, displays the address of the active Web page.

Archive To back up files and store them somewhere other than the main hard drive.

CD-R Another name for a CD-ROM disc.

CD-ROM The acronym for Compact Disc-Read Only Memory; an optical storage device used to permanently store data and from which you can read and open files.

CD-RW A compact disc that can be reused to read and save files.

Click To press the left (or primary) mouse button once.

Clipboard A temporary storage area in Windows that stores the most recently copied item.

Close button The button in a title bar that closes a window or a program.

Collapse button A small minus (–) button to the left of a folder that you click to hide the items in that folder.

Compress A process to reduce the size of a file.

Context-sensitive command A command associated with activities in which you are engaged; often activated by right-clicking a screen item.

Desktop The basic screen from which Windows and programs are run, and which consists of program icons, a taskbar, a Start button, and a mouse pointer.

Dialog box A box that asks you to make a decision about an individual object or topic. Dialog boxes do not have Minimize buttons.

Double-click The action of clicking the left mouse button twice in rapid succession while keeping the mouse still.

Drag The action of moving something from one location on the screen to another; the action of dragging includes releasing the mouse button at the desired time or location.

Drive An area of storage that is formatted with the Windows file system and that has a drive letter such as C.

Edit mode A Windows mode that enables you to change the name of a file or folder, and works the same in all Windows programs.

Expand button A small plus (+) button to the left of a folder that you click to display the items in that folder.

File Data that you save and store on a drive, such as a Word document or a PowerPoint presentation.

File extension The characters to the right of the period in a file name, and that tell the computer the program to use to open the file; extensions can be displayed or hidden.

Flash drive A small, portable, digital storage device that connects to a computer's USB port; also called a thumb drive, jump drive, or USB drive.

Floppy disk drive (or floppy drive) The original storage device for a microcomputer, which enables portable, permanent storage on floppy disks.

Folder A storage area, represented on the screen by a picture of a paper file folder, used to store files or other folders.

Graphical user interface (GUI) A computer interface with which you interact with the computer through the use of graphics and point-and-click technology; GUIs show documents as they will look in their final form.

Hard drive A large disk drive inside your computer, also referred to as a Local Disk.

Horizontal scroll bar The bar at the bottom of a window that enables you to move left and right to view information that extends beyond the left and right edges of the screen.

Icon A graphic representation of an object that you can click to open that object.

Left pane In the My Computer window, a pane at the left that displays information and commonly used tools.

Local Disk A large disk drive inside your computer, also referred to as a hard disk.

Maximize To increase the size of a window to fill the screen.

Menu A list of commands within a category.

Menu bar The bar beneath the title bar that lists the names of menu categories.

Minimize Removing the window from the screen without closing it; minimized windows can be reopened by clicking the associated button in the taskbar.

Mouse pointer The arrow, I-beam, or other symbol that shows the location or position of the mouse on your screen; also called the pointer.

My Computer A window that gives you access to the files and folders on your computer.

Notification area The area on the right side of the taskbar that keeps you informed about processes that are occurring in the background, such as antivirus software, network connections, and other utility programs; also displays the time.

Operating system A set of instructions that coordinates the activities of your computer; Microsoft Windows XP is an operating system.

Paint A Windows program in which graphics are created or edited.

Pointer See mouse pointer.

Pointing Positioning the tip of the pointer in the center of an icon or other screen object.

Quick Launch toolbar An area to the right of the Start button that contains shortcut icons for commonly used programs.

Recycle Bin A storage area for files that have been deleted; files can be recovered from the Recycle Bin or permanently removed.

Restore Using the Restore Down button to return a window to the size it was before it was maximized.

Right-click The action of clicking the right mouse button.

ScreenTip A small box that displays useful information when you perform various mouse actions such as pointing to screen elements or dragging.

Scroll box The box in the vertical and horizontal scroll bars that can be dragged to reposition the document on the screen.

Shortcut menu A context-sensitive menu that displays commands and options relevant to the selected object.

Sizing handle A small square or circle in the corners and the middle of the sides of a graphic that can be used to increase or decrease the size of the graphic.

Start button The button on the left side of the taskbar that is used to start programs, change system settings, find Windows help, or shut down the computer.

Status area Another name for the notification area on the right side of the taskbar.

Submenu A second-level menu activated by selecting a menu option.

System tray Another name for the notification area on the right side of the taskbar.

Task pane A pane that opens on the side of a window that is used to display commonly used tools.

Taskbar The area of the screen that displays the Start button and the name of any open documents. The taskbar may also display shortcut buttons for other programs.

Thumb drive A small storage device that plugs into a computer USB port; also called a USB drive or a flash drive.

Thumbnail A miniature representation of the contents of a picture file.

Title bar Displays the program icon, the name of the document, and the name of the program. The Minimize, Maximize/Restore Down, and Close buttons are grouped on the right side of the title bar.

Toolbars Rows of buttons, usually located under a menu bar, from which you can perform commands using a single click.

USB drive A small storage device that plugs into a computer USB port; also called a thumb drive or a flash drive.

Vertical scroll bar The bar at the right side of a window that enables you to move up and down to view information that extends beyond the top and bottom of the screen.

Wildcard A character, such as an asterisk, that can be used to match any number of characters in a file search.

Window A box or screen that displays information or a program. Windows usually consist of title bars, toolbars, menu bars, and status bars. A window will always have a Minimize button and a Close button.

Windows When spelled with a capital *W*, refers to the operating system that runs your computer.

Wordpad A simple word processing program that comes with Windows XP.

Index

SINGLE PC LICENSE AGREEMENT AND LIMITED WARRANTY

READ THIS LICENSE CAREFULLY BEFORE OPENING THIS PACKAGE. BY OPENING THIS PACKAGE, YOU ARE AGREEING TO THE TERMS AND CONDITIONS OF THIS LICENSE. IF YOU DO NOT AGREE, DO NOT OPEN THE PACKAGE. PROMPTLY RETURN THE UNOPENED PACKAGE AND ALL ACCOMPANYING ITEMS TO THE PLACE YOU OBTAINED THEM. *THESE TERMS APPLY TO ALL LICENSED SOFTWARE ON THE DISK EXCEPT THAT THE TERMS FOR USE OF ANY SHAREWARE OR FREEWARE ON THE DISKETTES ARE AS SET FORTH IN THE ELECTRONIC LICENSE LOCATED ON THE DISK:*

1. GRANT OF LICENSE and OWNERSHIP: The enclosed computer programs ("Software") are licensed, not sold, to you by Prentice-Hall, Inc. ("We" or the "Company") and in consideration of your purchase or adoption of the accompanying Company textbooks and/or other materials, and your agreement to these terms. We reserve any rights not granted to you. You own only the disk(s) but we and/or our licensors own the Software itself. This license allows you to use and display your copy of the Software on a single computer (i.e., with a single CPU) at a single location for academic use only, so long as you comply with the terms of this Agreement. You may make one copy for back up, or transfer your copy to another CPU, provided that the Software is usable on only one computer.

2. RESTRICTIONS: You may not transfer or distribute the Software or documentation to anyone else. Except for backup, you may not copy the documentation or the Software. You may not network the Software or otherwise use it on more than one computer or computer terminal at the same time. You may not reverse engineer, disassemble, decompile, modify, adapt, translate, or create derivative works based on the Software or the Documentation. You may be held legally responsible for any copying or copyright infringement which is caused by your failure to abide by the terms of these restrictions.

3. TERMINATION: This license is effective until terminated. This license will terminate automatically without notice from the Company if you fail to comply with any provisions or limitations of this license. Upon termination, you shall destroy the Documentation and all copies of the Software. All provisions of this Agreement as to limitation and disclaimer of warranties, limitation of liability, remedies or damages, and our ownership rights shall survive termination.

4. DISCLAIMER OF WARRANTY: THE COMPANY AND ITS LICENSORS MAKE NO WARRANTIES ABOUT THE SOFTWARE, WHICH IS PROVIDED "AS-IS." IF THE DISK IS DEFECTIVE IN MATERIALS OR WORKMANSHIP, YOUR ONLY REMEDY IS TO RETURN IT TO THE COMPANY WITHIN 30 DAYS FOR REPLACEMENT UNLESS THE COMPANY DETERMINES IN GOOD FAITH THAT THE DISK HAS BEEN MISUSED OR IMPROPERLY INSTALLED, REPAIRED, ALTERED OR DAMAGED. THE COMPANY DISCLAIMS ALL WARRANTIES, EXPRESS OR IMPLIED, INCLUDING WITHOUT LIMITATION, THE IMPLIED WARRANTIES OF MERCHANTABILITY AND FITNESS FOR A PARTICULAR PURPOSE. THE COMPANY DOES NOT WARRANT, GUARANTEE OR MAKE ANY REPRESENTATION REGARDING THE ACCURACY, RELIABILITY, CURRENTNESS, USE, OR RESULTS OF USE, OF THE SOFTWARE.

5. LIMITATION OF REMEDIES AND DAMAGES: IN NO EVENT, SHALL THE COMPANY OR ITS EMPLOYEES, AGENTS, LICENSORS OR CONTRACTORS BE LIABLE FOR ANY INCIDENTAL, INDIRECT, SPECIAL OR CONSEQUENTIAL DAMAGES ARISING OUT OF OR IN CONNECTION WITH THIS LICENSE OR THE SOFTWARE, INCLUDING, WITHOUT LIMITATION, LOSS OF USE, LOSS OF DATA, LOSS OF INCOME OR PROFIT, OR OTHER LOSSES SUSTAINED AS A RESULT OF INJURY TO ANY PERSON, OR LOSS OF OR DAMAGE TO PROPERTY, OR CLAIMS OF THIRD PARTIES, EVEN IF THE COMPANY OR AN AUTHORIZED REPRESENTATIVE OF THE COMPANY HAS BEEN ADVISED OF THE POSSIBILITY OF SUCH DAMAGES. SOME JURISDICTIONS DO NOT ALLOW THE LIMITATION OF DAMAGES IN CERTAIN CIRCUMSTANCES, SO THE ABOVE LIMITATIONS MAY NOT ALWAYS APPLY.

6. GENERAL: THIS AGREEMENT SHALL BE CONSTRUED IN ACCORDANCE WITH THE LAWS OF THE UNITED STATES OF AMERICA AND THE STATE OF NEW YORK, APPLICABLE TO CONTRACTS MADE IN NEW YORK, AND SHALL BENEFIT THE COMPANY, ITS AFFILIATES AND ASSIGNEES. This Agreement is the complete and exclusive statement of the agreement between you and the Company and supersedes all proposals, prior agreements, oral or written, and any other communications between you and the company or any of its representatives relating to the subject matter. If you are a U.S. Government user, this Software is licensed with "restricted rights" as set forth in subparagraphs (a)-(d) of the Commercial Computer-Restricted Rights clause at FAR 52.227-19 or in subparagraphs (c)(1)(ii) of the Rights in Technical Data and Computer Software clause at DFARS 252.227-7013, and similar clauses, as applicable.

Should you have any questions concerning this agreement or if you wish to contact the Company for any reason, please contact in writing:

Multimedia Production
Higher Education Division
Prentice-Hall, Inc.
1 Lake Street
Upper Saddle River NJ 07458